William Lloyd Garrison

and the Challenge
of Emancipation

American Biographical History Series

SERIES EDITORS

Alan M. Kraut, *The American University*
Jon L. Wakelyn, *The Catholic University of America*

ADVISORY EDITOR

Arthur S. Link, *Princeton University*

William Lloyd Garrison

and the Challenge of Emancipation

James Brewer Stewart
Macalester College

Harlan Davidson, Inc.
Arlington Heights, Illinos 60004

Library of Congress
Cataloging-in-Publication Data
Stewart, James Brewer
   William Lloyd Garrison and the challenge
of emancipation / James B. Stewart
   p. cm.—(The American biographical
history series)
Includes bibliographical references and
index.
ISBN 0-88295-885-2
1. Garrison, William Lloyd, 1805–1879. 2.
Abolitionists—United States—Biography. 3.
Slavery—United States—Anti-slavery
movements. I. Title. II. Series.
E449.G25S74   1992
322.4'4'092—dc20
[B]   91-14260
                                          CIP

Book design: Roger Eggers
Cover portrait and frontispiece courtesy of
North Wind Picture Archives.

Manufactured in the United States of
America
96   95   94   93   92   1   2   3   4   5
MG

As biographies offer access to the past, they reflect the needs of the present. Newcomers to biography and biographical history often puzzle over the plethora of books that some lives inspire. "Why do we need so many biographies of Abraham Lincoln?" they ask, as they search for the "correct" version of the sixteenth president's story. Each generation needs to revisit Lincoln because each generation has fresh questions, inspired by its own experiences. Collectively, the answers to these questions expand our understanding of Lincoln and America in the 1860s, but they also assist us to better comprehend our own time. People concerned with preserving such civil liberties as freedom of the press in time of national crisis have looked at Lincoln's approach to political opposition during and after secession. Civil rights activists concerned with racial injustice have turned to Lincoln's life to clarify unresolved social conflicts that persist more than a century after his assassination.

Useful as it is to revisit such lives, it is equally valuable to explore those often neglected by biographers. Almost always, biographies are written about prominent individuals who changed, in some measure, the world around them. But who is prominent and what constitutes noteworthy change are matters of debate. Historical beauty is definitely in the eye of the beholder. That most American biographies tell of great white males and their untainted accomplishments speaks volumes about the society that produced such uncritical paeans. More recently, women and men of various racial, religious, and economic backgrounds have expanded the range of American biography. The lives of prominent African-American leaders, Native American chieftains, and immigrant sweatshop workers who climbed the success ladder to its top now crowd onto those library shelves next to familiar figures.

In the American Biographical History Series, specialists in key areas of American history describe the lives of important men and women of many different races, religions, and ethnic backgrounds as those figures shaped and were shaped by the political, social, economic, and cultural issues of their day and the people with whom they lived. Biographical subjects and readers share a dialogue across time and space as biographers pose the questions suggested by life in modern-day America to those who lived in other eras. Each life offers a timeless reservoir of answers to questions from the present. The result is at once edifying and entertaining.

The concise biographical portrait found in each volume in this series is enriched and made especially instructive by the attention paid to generational context. Each biographer has taken pains to link his or her subject to peers and predecessors engaged in the same area of accomplishment. Even the rare individuals whose ideas or behavior transcend their age operated within a broad social context of values, attitudes, and beliefs. Iconoclastic radicals, too, whatever their era, owed a debt to earlier generations of protesters and left a legacy for those who would resist the status quo in the future.

Biographers in the series offer readers new companions, individuals of accomplishment, whose lives and works can be weighed and assessed and consulted as resources in answering the nagging questions that the thoughtful in every generation ask of the past to better comprehend the present. The makers of America—male and female, black and white and red and yellow, Christian, Moslem, Jew, atheist, agnostic, and polytheist, rich and poor and in between—all testify with their lives that the past is prologue. Anxious to share his rich experiences with those willing to listen, an elderly Eastern European immigrant living in Pittsburgh boasted, "By myself, I'm a book!" He, too, realized that an important past could be explicated through the narrative of a life, in fact, his own.

When a biographer sees his or her subject in broader context, important themes are crystallized, an era is illuminated. The single life becomes a window to a past age and its truths for succeeding generations and for you.

ALAN M. KRAUT
JON L. WAKELYN

For Dottie

CONTENTS

INTRODUCTION AND ACKNOWLEDGMENTS

To most of his contemporaries, the name of William Lloyd Garrison carried implications of revolution. From the 1830s until the conclusion of the Civil War, Garrison demanded that the South's three million slaves be emancipated immediately, that women be accorded equality in public life, that the nation's system of racial segregation and legal discrimination be dismantled, that America's dominant values be transformed to secure the liberation of all humanity. Denounced by most as a dangerous fanatic but revered by his followers as a far-seeing prophet, Garrison virtually embodied America's first great movements for social justice.

This brief biography attempts, above all, to suggest the value of Garrison's career for his generation, and for ours. In Garrison's lifetime, as in ours, white Americans fundamentally denied their professions of democracy by condoning pervasive racial oppression. Then, as now, women and men, both black and white, contested over deeply conflicting interpretations of Jefferson's assertion that "all men are created equal." In foreseeing the possible catastrophe of civil war, Garrison's generation struggled much as we do to insure that peaceful mechanisms of just governance might prevail against mindless destruction. And like the best of us, Garrison led others to find transcendent meanings in their own lives by resisting oppressors and challenging the apathetic. His choices were often flawed as well as inspired, and like us he found himself both empowered and limited by the circumstances of his age. For all these reasons, the biography of William Lloyd Garrison offers insights into a vital chapter in the American past, one with rich legacies for our time as well.

Many generous, intelligent people have helped me to improve this biography. Garrison's modern biographers, John L. Thomas, Walter Merrill, Russell B. Nye, and R. Jackson Wilson supplied important perspectives that have greatly influenced my own. John McKivigan, Don Jacobs, Frederick Blue, and Deborah Van Broekhoven, all accomplished scholars of abolitionism, offered challenging criticisms and saved me from errors of facts and diction. Arthur Link, Harlan Davidson's general editor for history, offered important suggestions on style and presentation. Alan Kraut, co-editor of this biography series, deserves special thanks for unstinting gifts of wisdom, encouragement, learning, and common sense. Sister James Theresa of the College of St. Catherine's has my gratitude for providing so hospitable a place to write.

Macalester College offers an environment peculiarly rich in resources for scholarship. The stipend attached to my position as James Wallace Professor of History gave invaluable research support for this book. Talented and critical Macalester colleagues—Peter Rachleff, Leslie Vaughn, and Donald Culverson—inspired me to rethink and rewrite. Macalester's DeWitt Wallace Library, capacious, comfortable, and managed by talented staff, put many necessary reference works within easy reach. Macalester's president, Bob Gavin, arranged to defray the cost of manuscript preparation and, more important, also read every page with a critical discernment that confirms the high vision of his academic leadership.

In completing my fourth book, I am more convinced than ever that Dorothy C. Stewart is as gifted an editor as any author could wish to encounter. She has vastly improved my style, and whatever is appealing in the "voice" of this book is due in large measure to her. Beyond her grasp of syntax, she also challenged my assumptions and questioned the soundness of my logic time and again, demanding a standard of intellectual clarity that I have, I hope, in some sense met. For all this, and for so much more that is comprehended by our twenty-five-year partnership, I dedicate this book, with love, to her.

Statue of William Lloyd Garrison (bronze), Boston, Mass. *(Courtesy North Wind Picture Archives)*

CHAPTER ONE

Tragedy

Abjah Garrison tippled frequently with his seafaring comrades, and perhaps more than his companions he felt he had good reasons for seeking solace in rum and conviviality. When he and his young family had first arrived in 1805 from Nova Scotia at the seaport of Newburyport, Massachusetts, commerce was brisk, and he quickly began to prosper as a sailing master. "There are more than fifty ways you might find employment here," he had assured those he had left behind. Commercial voyages by Abjah to places like Virginia, the West Indies, and Labrador provided the Garrisons a good living at first and gave him the pride of satisfying labor. Just as important, seafaring also released the easygoing Abjah from the exacting expectations of his deeply pious, strong-willed wife Fanny.

By the summer of 1808, however, the shipping business in Newburyport harbor had all but ceased because naval war between England and France had prompted President Jefferson to lay an embargo against all foreign commerce by United States vessels. Abjah's means of livelihood had vanished, along with his means of escape. Meanwhile, family tragedy compounded his difficulties. In the spring of 1808, five-year-old Caroline, his eldest daughter, succumbed to an agonizing death caused by eating poisonous flower petals discarded by a neighbor. The birth of another daughter, Maria Elizabeth, two months later promised only more complication and discouragement, not a renewal of paternal hope. Then, too, there was Fanny's impromptu lecturing on religion and her preoccupation with prayer meetings and church affairs. Ultimately Abjah could be found more often than not over a jug in the alehouse or down at the wharves with his cronies.

Frances Maria (Fanny) Garrison met the stresses of mourning, childbearing, and penury with a faith that Abjah could never wholly fathom. For her, these crises, like all of life's crises, required a redoubled belief in the redemptive powers of Jesus, expressed in a consuming Baptist piety. Hers was a powerful evangelical creed, as Abjah well knew, and Fanny had always served it even at the risk of estrangement from kin and family. She had been raised a staunch Anglican in Nova Scotia by a father who tolerated no challenge to his authority. In adolescence, however, Fanny was converted, or "saved," by an itinerant Baptist preacher, one of the many evangelical zealots who stirred the fires of religious revivalism in the Northeast just before the American Revolution. Her newfound faith required henceforth that she testify constantly to her spiritual rebirth, thereby seeking "conversion" in others by convincing them of their personal guilt and of Jesus' saving power. Fanny's outraged father demanded that she recant, and when she adamantly refused, he banished her from the family. Refusing reconciliation with her parents on any terms but her own, she went to live with an aunt who shared her religious zeal.

In 1797 she first met the handsome, ambitious Abjah at a Baptist prayer meeting and soon eagerly accepted the security, respectability, and escape to a promising future which he embodied. In turn Fanny, who was tall, sharp-featured, with jet black hair and a quick tongue, doubtless offered Abjah the promise of a strong, reliable helpmeet. Seldom, however, would a marriage bring together two such conflicting temperaments. Perhaps Fanny had expected to "redeem" her husband after the wedding by inspiring in him a religious conversion much like her own. Unfortunately, she had actually married a young man whose spasmodic efforts to grasp salvation would always be overcome by wanderlust and sociability, and who would soon come to resent her pleas that he change his basic nature. If Abjah, on the other hand, had expected his new

wife to tolerate his love of good times while cheerfully keepi.
house, he, too, had been sorely mistaken. He had actually mai
a young woman determined at all costs to live out the demands
her Lord, Abjah's contrary inclinations, hopes, or expectations no
withstanding.

The marriage ended in the summer of 1808, soon after the
death of Caroline and just after the birth of Elizabeth, when
William Lloyd was three years old and his older brother James
was seven. Fanny, dispirited by bereavement, exhausted by
childbirth, and troubled by her husband, entered the parlor of
her small house one afternoon and found Abjah and his comrades settling in for another visit of drink and aimless talk.
Choked by sudden anger, she seized the bottles, declared that
she would no longer tolerate such dissolution or permit her
home to be used as a dramshop, and ejected them all. Later that
day Abjah returned only long enough to collect his possessions
and left his family forever.

Whether or not Fanny castigated herself for failing in her
Christian duty to save her husband and unite her family can
never be known. But from the moment of Abjah's departure,
she set herself to insuring that the sins of the vanished father not
visit themselves upon her children. Through religious instruction and personal inspiration she would lead James, Lloyd, and
Elizabeth to learn obedience to the requirements of Christian
conscience. Thus inspired and restrained, they would learn
never to permit themselves to reenact Abjah's disgraceful fall
into worldly self-indulgence and spiritual bankruptcy. Throughout his life Lloyd would always insist that he remembered very
little about his father. Perhaps this absence of memory was encouraged by Fanny's determination to obliterate Abjah's example. Certainly it could be argued that his lifetime struggle to
achieve spiritual sanctification and worldly recognition originated in Abjah's flight from family, religion, and social responsibility.

Fanny soon discovered that the day-to-day demands of survival competed with her efforts to direct her children's develop-

ment in the faith. To earn money she was forced to leave James, Lloyd, and Elizabeth each day, hiring herself out as a nurse. This really meant performing the lowest domestic labor, "slavish work" in her own view that she resented deeply. Her bitterness was compounded by the knowledge that Abjah's "fall" had now precipitated her own loss of respectability; she was now a deserted wife, fully recognized as such throughout Newburyport's tightly constructed social order. Once, her now-disgraced husband had contracted "honorably" for his services with the town's commercial elite—the Cushings, Lowells, and Jacksons, whose fine Georgian brick houses, Anglophile tastes, and Federalist politics marked them among the "first families" of the Commonwealth. But now, Fanny nursed their sick, emptied their slop jars, cleaned their linens and, when desperate, even sent her children to beg scraps from their tables. She tried to protect her dignity by resisting any high-handedness and setting clear limits, as when one of her employers treated her like "dirt hardly fit to walk on." Fanny gave her mistress immediate notice along with "a piece of my mind," telling her forthrightly "I would not set [you] with the dogs of my father's flock." These proud retorts also conveyed Fanny's deep and lifelong envy of those of high station. As her letters make clear, she was happiest at work when other servants treated her "like a lady" on orders from employers who seemed to regard her as their equal. Admiring the graceful furniture and tasteful landscaping of the homes in which she labored, Fanny's yearnings for things worldly and the respectability to which they attested coexisted uneasily with her zeal to express her spirituality.

It is not clear whether Fanny attempted to shield her children from her complex feelings of envy and insecurity. Lloyd, at any rate, seems never to have complained when directed to sell apples or molasses candy on the street, or to walk past jeering playmates, tin pan in hand, to collect left-overs from the wealthy kitchens up on High Street. It is telling, however, that in later years Garrison was eager to recount detailed memories of his childhood deprivation and lack of education, claiming that his earliest struggles against poverty had furnished him a fortunate starting point for his rise to national prominence as a foe of corruption and licentiousness. Though unable to recall his father in person, Garrison would struggle throughout his life to prove to himself and others that he had overcome the humiliation of Abjah's impoverished legacy.

Because of her determined approach to adversity, it was said that "only a cannonball could kill Fanny Garrison." Still her family's poverty tested her sorely. Despite her resolve to retain control over her children, she was soon forced for economic reasons to split up her family. In 1812 she moved to Lynn, Massachusetts, with James, her eldest, leaving Lloyd and Elizabeth in Newburyport with friends. In Lynn, a bustling center of shoemakers, she hoped to find work for herself and a good apprenticeship for James. But soon after her arrival she felt her guilt compounding over her decision to leave her children. "Know that I am here in Lynn seeking living for my children," she wrote defensively to her Newburyport friends. "I do not like Lynn but necessity compels me to stay in it."

Prompted by these feelings, Fanny made careful arrangements to insure Lloyd's Christian nurturing. Though she was absent, he remained enveloped in her morally charged spiritual world. Even before her departure for Lynn, when Fanny had begun working as a nurse, her closest friends the Farnhams had provided her children with an environment where her strong piety held sway. "Aunt Martha" Farnham, a deeply devout Baptist, was the wife of David Farnham, a ship captain with whom the Garrisons had shared housing upon their arrival in Newburyport. They maintained a household filled with hymn singing and prayer. Elizabeth remained with the Farnhams after Fanny and James had moved to Lynn. Lloyd, however, was placed in still another "faithful" home, that of Ezekial Bartlett, a poor woodcutter and spiritual leader (deacon) of Fanny's church, and his wife, Elizabeth, one of Fanny's closest friends and spiritual communicants. Lloyd's nurturing in the faith of his mother went forward with barely a pause.

The Bartletts cared little for Lloyd's education, which lagged badly and was usually sacrificed for the performance of household chores. By his own recollections, he was never taught proper grammar or spelling, which he later learned on his own. Because he was left-handed, his schoolmaster also neglected teaching him a proper script. His extraordinarily legible "hand" (a delight for contemporaries and for historians since) again resulted from his later, unaided efforts. But in matters of the spirit, the Bartletts schooled him well. Lloyd sang in the choir, retaining throughout his life the exact lyrics of hundreds of hymns. With Deacon Bartlett to instruct him, he listened carefully to sermons, read juvenile religious tracts, and prepared his Sunday school lessons. In adulthood, he was to claim complete reading knowledge of only one book, the King James Bible, which he would quote with much greater frequency and accuracy than any other source.

Fanny, meanwhile, sought by letters from Lynn to retain her son's concern and emotional dependence:

> My mind is all hurry and perturbation, tired with slavish work, tired with vain interrogation and altercations on caprice and folly— O that I could once more be returned to my friends again and have just enough to supply my real Want—with my tender offspring around me in the company of my Dear Christian Friends—And my mind engaged in religion—Happy thoughts, though visionary at present.

"I am homesick," she lamented in closing, instructing her eight-year-old to "write and let me know whether my children are dead or alive." Lloyd, understandably, responded as any young child would. He missed her deeply and once, after quarrelling with Deacon Bartlett, tried running away. Taking a companion, he headed for Lynn, only to be overhauled and returned to his custodians.

Because he felt her absence so keenly, Lloyd strove all the more to meet his mother's expectations. Without the presence of a father, moreover, or even the conscious memory of one,

Lloyd's only role model was his mother, making it difficult to resist Fanny's demands, even should he have tried. Reinforced by his zealous caretakers, he learned early to obey the inner voice of Christian conscience and to regulate his behavior by conforming to godly principles. By so doing he also learned that he could earn both his mother's loving approval and assurance of salvation. Lloyd's displays of self-control and piety, in turn, alleviated some of her deeper insecurities by confirming her maternal dominion; thanks to her influence, Lloyd would never abandon himself to worldly excess, as Abjah had done.

In her older son James, however, Fanny's attempts at domination prompted only wholesale defiance. By fourteen, he had succumbed to violent alcoholism and sexual excess. James had been seven when Abjah had fled, and unlike Lloyd remembered his father clearly. Perhaps his compulsions arose from anxieties that he, somehow, had been responsible for his father's devastating absence. Perhaps, too, he wished subconsciously to punish Fanny (and all women) not only for her part in Abjah's desertion, but also for her ceaseless efforts to erase his memory of his father by making him exclusively into his mother's son. Whatever the reasons for James's rage, it shattered forever Fanny's hopes that he, like Lloyd, would prove himself "a good boy and a great comfort to me." Instead, he inflicted on her contemptuous abuse, followed always by self-abasing pleas for her forgiveness. For Fanny, such behavior forced her to confront the most terrible realization she could imagine. Even as she strove to secure her sons' Christian obedience, James was displaying tenfold the sins for which she had driven her husband away.

Abjah had tippled, but James drank to stupification and fits of violence. Abjah had been morally lax but probably not wanton. James by fourteen had already seduced "a lovely little girl" about his own age and had involved at least one other young woman in a debauch "until [they] went home in a state of brutal intoxication." Abjah had shamed Fanny and had forfeited her "respectable" station. James tortured her with gruesome public humiliation, as when, naked and drunk, he and a friend hid in a

field of tall grass and then sprang out to terrify a group of passing schoolgirls. "I was amazing everybody who came my way,"
he recalled of another drunken display, "insulting the girls with
most obscene language, and they had to send for my master to
take me away." By 1815, when Fanny was able to reassemble all
her children in Lynn, James had already gone far in rejecting all
the pious relationships and reassuring Christian precepts that
Lloyd now valued so highly. Though Lloyd had sorely missed
Fanny while living with the Bartletts, their household had nevertheless supplied him with day-to-day security and spiritual assurance. But now actually living with James's terrible behavior
must have left him shocked, confused, and terribly threatened
as he watched his mother struggle to contain the upheavals that
overwhelmed them all. To Lloyd, James's madness revealed as
nothing else could the demons that must have tortured his father
as well.

Before the unworldly eyes of his younger brother Lloyd,
James repeatedly returned home, haggard, dissipated, and
sometimes bloody, consumed by remorse and begging his mother's forgiveness. After tears and lamenting supplications, Fanny,
in desperation, invariably tried to ease his distress. She would
pay off his creditors, defend him to his employers, and attempt
to give him a "clean slate" by dipping into her scant savings and
arranging for one more apprenticeship. By so doing, Fanny
hoped vainly to nurture in James a rekindled spark of Christian
conscience and self-control. For the same reason she beseeched
him to reform, not in angry tones, but "in an affectionate, kind
manner." James's behavior, she earnestly counselled, was ruin-
ing his health, destroying his reputation, and causing his deeply
loving mother "many sufferings." Most of all, as James would
later recall, she appealed that he was risking "the damnation of
[his] soul in the world to come," and that spiritual rebirth would
be his only by accepting Christ's atonement for his sins. Invariably, James promised to "do better." Inevitably, Fanny's
method of excusing, supporting, and pleading only inflamed his
guilt and led him again to dissipation. The repeating cycle of

pathology could only cause Lloyd to hate all the more James's self-destructive passions and their devastating impact on his family.

In October 1815, Fanny's employer, Paul Newhall, persuaded her to move to Baltimore, where he planned to establish a new shoe factory. Though Lloyd, small and frail, found shoemaking very taxing, Fanny welcomed Newhall's proposal, which seemed to offer the beleaguered Garrisons a fresh start—apprenticeships for the boys, boarding for the family at Newhall's home, and neighbors that harbored no memories of "Crazy Jem" Garrison, as some now called James. But once aboard the ship to Baltimore, the family saw its troubles erupt once again. While Fanny nursed the chronically seasick Lloyd, James mixed freely with the sailors. Their work fascinated him, and so did their easy access to the rum locker. Like Abjah, he began sensing in the swaying deck beneath him a means to break free from his painful relationship with Fanny and his failure to meet society's expectations. Fanny debarked in Baltimore anticipating a fresh start. Her hopes, thanks to James, went glimmering even as she entertained them.

Briefly it seemed otherwise. Though Paul Newhall's factory opened only to close soon after, Fanny's initial circumstances were still promising. She began working as a nurse-housekeeper for a wealthy family, the Dorseys, who were related to the prominent Federalist Timothy Pickering. Mr. Dorsey also agreed to sponsor James as an apprentice, while Lloyd helped his mother by running errands and doing light chores. She especially enjoyed her work once she discovered that the Dorseys treated her and her children with respect, providing generously for them and insisting that their other servants defer to her superior status. Reassured for the moment of her social dignity, Fanny also threw herself into Baptist church affairs. She founded and directed Baltimore's first female prayer meeting and each week took her children to three Sunday services. It seemed, as she wrote to her Newburyport friends, that hard times were finally ending. James was quick to shatter her illusions.

Fanny and her employers began fighting over James's inability to keep an apprenticeship, thanks to his drinking. Soon she, too, had been dismissed and now wrote bitterly of the "great trial" to which James was submitting her, as when one of James's masters tried to give him a "sound drubbing" for his misbehavior. James attacked first and then, as he later wrote, "made my escape, and flew to my mother for protection." Ashamed and still defiant, he next left Baltimore to fill a clerk's position in Frederick. There he lagged for his lack of mathematical skills, further perfected "the habit of getting drunk," harassed some schoolchildren, brandished loaded pistols, and finally threatened his master with a knife. Back he then crawled to his "poor mother," who gave him "the only fourteen dollars she had in the world" in exchange for his vows to return to Lynn, to resume shoemaking, and to drink no more. "I promised to do better," James wrote of what proved to be his final departure from his mother, "and left my parent in tears for the wellfare [sic] of her ruined son. I shall never forget that parting. It seemed my heart would burst, but I could not shed a tear."

The road to Lynn never led James back to Fanny Garrison. It directed him next to the Salem wharves and to seafaring, his father's only sure means of escape. Unlike Abjah, however, James would finally return. Twenty-five years later, devastated by a lifetime of torments, James appeared at Lloyd's home to seek the solace and forgiveness that would let him die in peace.

In 1816, however, Lloyd could never have imagined such a reconciliation. As James's dissolution again overwhelmed the family, Lloyd found his circumstances unbearable. Every element in his eleven-year upbringing made him loathe the emotional chaos which entangled him once more. His situation grew all the more intolerable because as James failed, Fanny increasingly looked to Lloyd to supply the family with stability and vindicate her efforts as a Christian mother. "He is a fine boy, though he is mine," Fanny wrote about Lloyd in the spring of 1816 as her troubles with James compounded. "Every Sunday he goes to the Baptist [church] although he has so far to walk. I expect he will be a complete Baptist as to tenets...I do hope he will always be so steady."

Finally Lloyd could stand no more. Even as his mother and James were struggling toward their inevitable parting, he decided he must return alone to Newburyport to start life, at eleven, on his own. In making his own choice to leave, Lloyd openly challenged Fanny's authority, but he did so without violating in any way her deeper maternal values. She had taught him always to act on the dictates of his inner convictions, and now he would do just that. In Newburyport he knew he could find relief from the turbulent family conflicts he so hated. Lloyd, like Fanny, also yearned for respectability and was deeply ashamed of his family's poverty and humiliation. In Newburyport he knew he could associate with stable, hard-working people who could help him to advance his education and prepare for an honorable career. "He is so discontented that he would leave me tomorrow and go with strangers to Newburyport," Fanny confessed in the spring of 1816. "He longs to go back to school...he can't mention any of you without tears."

In the fall of 1816, Lloyd made his return to Newburyport. Unlike his brother, he carried with him his mother's blessing. Fanny and Lloyd would remain physically apart for seven years, but in the meantime, by letter and prayer, she would continue her efforts to shape his will to hers. Lloyd, for his part, would begin exploring his deeply conflicting desires to retain the favor of God and his mother while seeking to triumph over his shameful origins with a measure of worldly success.

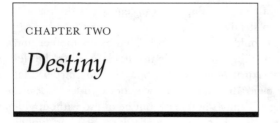

CHAPTER TWO

Destiny

Lloyd had not been long in Newburyport when Fanny began writing him once again to admonish and instruct. She had already fallen victim to tuberculosis and by 1821 was beginning to cough blood, leading her to focus all the more on the spiritual well-being of the only son remaining within her influence:

> Your good behavior will more than compensate for all my trouble; only let me hear that you are steady, and go not in the way of bad company, and my heart will be lifted up to God for you, that you may be kept from the snares and temptations of this evil world. Be a good boy and God will bless you, and you have a Mother, although distant from you, that loves you with tenderness.

Striking out on his own, young Garrison was understandably determined to make his own way in choosing a vocation and to pursue goals of his own devising. Yet letters like this one only made it all the harder for him to relinquish family memories, start afresh, and become a "self-made man." Fanny's warnings of the "snares and temptations of this evil world" certainly did not mesh easily with the secular maxims of Benjamin Franklin, the figure whose career Garrison now hoped to replicate.

Garrison, however, did know clearly what sort of position or apprenticeship his personal ambitions would require and was determined not to compromise with anyone. When Fanny tried to bring him back to Baltimore by arranging for a clerkship there, he refused. Clerking, he told her, would obligate him always to work for others, since he did not believe he could ever amass capital enough to set up his own business. When Deacon Bartlett then apprenticed him to a cabinetmaker in nearby Haverhill, Garrison found that cabinetmaking, like shoemaking, required grueling physical labor. At the end of six weeks, hating the work, he again upset his mother's plans for him and ran back to Newburyport. The cabinetmaker, helpless in the face of Garrison's stubbornness, released him from the arranged contract.

What Garrison wanted to find in an apprenticeship was not simply livelihood, but a vocation and perhaps even a destiny. Manual skills like carpentry or an underling's job like clerking opened no clear possibilities for gaining a position that would bring recognition and public distinction. Fanny, of course, wished him to settle for learning a skill that would provide good earnings. Lloyd, however, yearned for a true career. He wanted to find an apprenticeship from which he might someday earn an enviable reputation and exercise power, a station which his mother had always secretly envied and of which his father could only have dreamed.

In the fall of 1818, the thirteen-year-old Garrison finally found a situation that seemed to meet his requirements when Ephriam W. Allen, owner and editor of the staunchly Federalist *Newburyport Herald* took him on for a seven-year apprenticeship. As the careers of other prominent newspaper editors confirmed, publishing was a trade that could lead to a career of honor and influence. Garrison's youth coincided with a time when literacy was expanding rapidly, spurred by growing popular participation in several aspects of public life, particularly politics, commercial enterprise, literary production, and religion. Newspapers proliferated, amplifying the voices of politicians, providing readers with essential information, and claiming to act as servants of cultural uplift and public morality. From the moment Garrison entered the *Herald*'s composing room, he found himself challenged and excited as never before. Throughout his life, he always considered Allen's decision to hire him an act of Divine Providence.

Even the craft of printing fascinated him. Though so small at first that he had to stand on a fifty-six pound weight in order to reach the composition box, he mastered typesetting with astonishing speed. Soon he could set a thousand ems (individual type pieces) perfectly in an hour and could roll the presses without leaving a blemish on the page. "I have delighted in nothing more, as regards manual work, than the manipulation of types," he would comment the year before his death. Allen soon promoted Garrison to office foreman and made him responsible for setting up the paper's format and preparing it for printing.

Garrison now began seeking an education in deadly earnest. His fascination with linking small bits of metal into words, sentences, and paragraphs and then presenting them in print for public notice grew from a deeper realization that now drove his efforts at self-education. The finished product, the newspaper itself, could become an extended representation of his own personality, knowledge, convictions, self-image, and power of expression. Influence and respect could come to him as it did to all successful editors by succeeding in "selling himself." Above all else, fame as a journalist meant gaining the public's respect and participating fully in an ever-expanding "marketplace of ideas." Garrison had already been taught to value very highly the promptings of his own conscience and the correctness of his "purest" thoughts. Unusually confident in the worthiness of his own opinions, he now anticipated the day when a newspaper would bring his self-created presence to the public's notice, earning him approbation and power. In preparation, he began reading randomly but constantly, taking every opportunity to enrich his knowledge and thus improve his social position. He was now working harder and feeling happier than ever before.

Like most artisans, Garrison boarded with his master, Ephriam Allen, who valued the boy's omnivorous reading habits. Allen supplied him with works by Shakespeare and Marlowe, along with romantics such as Byron, Scott, and Shelley. Allen also kept a large collection of Federalist party literature, including broadsides by party luminaries like Fisher

Ames, Oliver Wolcott, Harrison Gray Otis, and Timothy Pickering, and backfiles of the *Herald* itself. These were political
scriptures for Newburyport's commercial elite, many of whom,
despite the moribund condition of their party, still proudly
called themselves "high" Federalists and welcomed a continu-
ance of pious New England's struggle against Jeffersonian atheism and disorganization. As he studied these writings, he
absorbed a political persuasion to which he was already closely
attuned. The passion and licentiousness that these Federalists
always condemned in their opponents and the purity and sober
virtue they imputed to themselves matched his religious convictions and his own detestation of moral disorder, drawn from his
family's turbulent history. High Federalism, in this sense, constituted a broad political commentary derived from Fanny Garrison's religious maxims.

While Allen supplied parts of Garrison's education, fellow artisans provided the rest. Garrison soon began making friends
with other Newburyport apprentices, who, like himself, were
anxious to better themselves by acquiring "practical knowledge." After joining their "Franklin Club," he often gathered
with other aspiring young men to debate timely subjects and exchange useful information. From one of these friends he picked
up a smattering of Latin. From a group with whom he regularly
met to read poetry and share original verses he acquired a lifelong love of versifying. Garrison admired most of all his master's oldest apprentice, Tobias Miller, whom he remembered in
later years as having been "a very Benjamin Franklin for his
good sense and axiomatic speech." Indeed the parallel between
his own situation and Franklin's mythical rise as a printer from
poverty to fame seemed indisputable to the young Garrison,
and he remembered it for a lifetime.

Unlike so many artisans, whose religious views often ran
toward deism or skepticism, Garrison remained completely serious about his orthodox religious standing. Personal sanctification was important for self-improvement, but vital for
salvation. The Bartletts and the Farnhams, spiritual mentors

from his childhood, lived close by the *Herald* offices, and Garrison saw them regularly. Without fail he also attended the Baptist church, although he did not formally join it, perhaps because Fanny was embroiled throughout much of his apprenticeship in a bitter dispute with that church that resulted in the suspension of her own membership. He also rejoined the choir and continued his study of sermons and tracts. But as he strenuously maintained his piety he also prepared for success by incorporating this faith into a more complex and worldly posture, one more fitting for an up-to-date Christian gentleman, a young man of taste and sensibility as well as spirituality.

He began spending his money on his wardrobe and his time on socializing. An acquaintance recalled him as "an exceedingly genteel young man, always neatly, and perhaps I might say even elegantly dressed, and in good taste, and was quite popular with the ladies." Another caught well Garrison's stylistic attempt to reconcile an air of sophistication and sociability with a sober Christianity, remembering him as a "handsome and attractive youth, unusually dignified in bearing for a man so young." Though still wholly committed to obey his mother's injunction to "remain steady and go not in the way of bad company," Garrison had begun to find himself drawn increasingly to "the snares and temptations of this evil world."

Whether Garrison felt conscious anger about Fanny's stringent requirements can never be known. The possibility that he did deeply resent her demands on a more general, less conscious level is suggested by his first published essay, a vigorous defense of remaining single, published in the *Herald* over Garrison's pseudonym, An Old Bachelor. Confident enough of his publishable literary skills but too unsure of his reputation to reveal his name to editor Allen, Garrison disguised his handwriting and identity in an essay that complained (as Abjah might have) that "women in this country are too much idealized and flattered. . . . Women generally feel their importance and use it without mercy." In his next letter, the Old Bachelor satirically retracted these views, explaining that he had been bullied into doing so by a fearsome Aunt Betty who read his original com-munication and then, "clenching her fists, came directly to-wards me *pugis et calcibus* and gave me one of the most terrible lectures I have ever witnessed. . .I shall never forget her frightful attitude and overwhelming eloquence; my blood already recoils at the recollection of it." This intimidating figure cannot be proven to represent any of the women who helped raise him. Neither can the Old Bachelor be claimed as Garrison's con-scious representation of his father. Yet the contrived dispute seems to echo all too fully the memories and suppositions from childhood that a "self-made" young man might well need to ex-press in the hope of putting them behind him.

A month later, An Old Bachelor turned from writing about domestic strife to fictionalized adventure. In so doing, Garrison may again have been giving public voice to his deeper anxieties through his choice of subject, a disaster at sea that is rich with possible associations. Aboard ship, late at night, the narrator is awakened by a violent crash. As the vessel sinks he quickly clam-bers into a lifeboat and with other survivors sets off in a terrible storm. Suddenly, an enormous wave washes over the lifeboat and the narrator, "an expert swimmer," seizes an oar and strikes off on his own to save himself:

> I heard the groans of my expiring companions re-echo over the vast expanse of waters, fainter and more faint, and then—all was silent! An awful and most horrible stillness reigned: I murmured against that Providence who had so wonderfully preserved my life before,— it was a moment of despair;—I thought, or fancied I thought, that one of my dying companions was grasping me with the strength of a giant, and endeavoring to draw me under with him—or that some terrible monster of the deep was swallowing me up in his terrific jaws—a cold tremor pervaded my whole frame—my head grew dizzy, and my senses were completely worked up to a frenzy—I ut-tered a piercing shriek, and swooned away.

He awakens on the beach, miraculously saved.

This story certainly reveals a market-conscious young writer addressing a topic of particular interest to a seacoast community like Newburyport. It has also been argued that this passage prefigures Garrison's abolitionist zeal by outlining his obedience to the dictates of Divine Providence, not the opinions of men. If so, however, Garrison's essay suggests the future only by looking backward to the spectre of his past, for dependence on Divine Protection and a rejection of society for salvation registers above all the powerful influence of Fanny Garrison. Beyond this, it is hardly necessary to claim Abjah or James as the "grasping companion" or the "terrible monster" in order to recognize a deep yearning to find release from the past in order to begin anew. The escape he invented in fiction, however, fell far outside the conventional examples recommended by Benjamin Franklin.

Whatever their deeper meanings, Garrison's early writings pleased his master. During the next year, Allen encouraged him to write often for publication. Young Caleb Cushing, already one of the town's prominent citizens and later a leading national politician, took over the *Herald* briefly in Allen's absence and paid a well-deserved tribute, in print, to the Old Bachelor for "having favored us with a number of esteemed and valuable communications." Thus fortified, Garrison wrote several articles during the remainder of his apprenticeship that testified to the extraordinary range of his self-acquired knowledge and his growing self-assurance as a stylist. He had been working hard on his education, and now it showed in articles advocating a stronger United States policy in Latin America, analyses of the Russo-Turkish War and the Holy Alliance, and even a short story about a fortune hunter. The first fruits of his success were now even ripe enough, he believed, that he could seek his mother's approval. "I feel absolutely astonished at the different subjects I have discussed and the style in which they are written," he wrote Fanny proudly in 1823. "Indeed it is altogether a matter of surprise that I have met with such signal success, seeing as I do not understand *one rule of grammar* and have a very inferior education." Although Garrison told Fanny about his Old Bachelor articles, he did not send her any of his published pieces. Perhaps he feared that she would discern some of their less apparent meanings.

Fanny's response to his ambitions certainly must have wounded him, for she firmly withheld the approval that Garrison so badly desired. While "pleased with the idea" of his writing for the public, "providing nothing wrong should result from it," Fanny said she wanted to read his essays herself before making her final judgment. "You must write me one of your pieces . . . and I will give you my opinion whether you are an old bachelor, or whether you are A.O.B., A may stand for Ass, and O. for Oaf and B. for Blockhead," signing this dispiriting letter "your mother until death." She followed it several months later with still another that admonished him that he was "now at an age where you are forming the character for life, a dangerous age. Shun every wish for the sake of your soul as well as the body . . . Oh Lloyd, if I was to hear and have reason to think you was unsteady it would break my heart. God Forbid!" Serious tension had now surfaced between a relentlessly spiritual and demanding mother and a son who deeply needed her approval, but who was also divided by his worldly ambition and his strivings for personal purity.

By this time Fanny was too self-involved to defer even in a small way to Lloyd's ambitions. Surveying her life in 1820, she lamented the "rude blast of misfortune" that had taught her all too well that "all my dreams of happiness in this life were chimerical . . . imbecility in themselves and illusive." Two years later, with Elizabeth's sudden death in 1822 at the age of nine, Fanny's family had all but vanished. Only Lloyd, far off in Newburyport, remained to occupy her attention, which she now intensified further still. "Only religion is perennial," she insisted, as it "fortifies the mind to support trouble, elevates the heart and its perpetuity has no end." Fanny had suffered grievously and long since the dissolution of her marriage. She had been no less the victim of her family's many tragedies than any of its other members, and perhaps more so. This final summing of her life's truest meaning was all that remained to sustain her. At this late hour, she would not slacken in her faith, especially while the state of her son's soul remained uncertain.

By the spring of 1823, seven years had passed since Fanny and Lloyd had seen one another. Several times she urged him to visit, once even sending with her letter some old clothes accompanied with the reminder that these might well be the last tokens of her love that Lloyd would ever receive. But Allen needed his help in the office, Lloyd told her, repeatedly postponing his plans for the visit. He doubtless knew that she had much more to say about his budding career as a newspaper writer. He was also reluctant to leave his work just when upcoming elections promised him new opportunities to build his reputation as a political partisan.

With the help of Caleb Cushing, who supplied him background readings, Garrison had now been writing frequently and confidently on a wide range of issues. In the spring of 1823, just when Fanny was asking him to visit, Massachusetts Federalists nominated for governor one of Garrison's heroes, Harrison Gray Otis. Using a new pseudonym, One of the People, Garrison contributed a series of articles supporting Otis's candidacy, zealously condemning the opposition as a "turbulent faction" that had rallied to a "rebellious standard." Campaigning for Otis took clear priority over a reunion with his mother. He waited for two months, publishing political articles, before even replying to Fanny's final appeal that he return to her in Baltimore. When he finally did write, he told he would visit only if she would personally request that editor Allen release him from duties. Fanny could have only concluded that he was less concerned with her than with his blossoming career at the *Herald*.

Finally Garrison decided to try once more to impress his skeptical mother with an account of his accomplishments. He was now "turning author," he wrote, letting his time be "swallowed up" by publishing "political pieces." With pride he reported that he was no longer an anonymous writer either, for news of his identity had spread through Newburyport, and "I am at last discovered to be the author... [it] has caused no little sensation in the town." Writing, he explained enthusiastically, insured that his "leisure moments" were being "usefully employed," for he was cultivating "the seeds of improvement in my breast, and expanding the intellectual... powers of my mind." He tried again to reassure her that he was not one of those "giddy youths" given to "wasting time in a dull, insipid manner," and he attempted, clumsily, to prompt her sympathetic understanding: "You will undoubtedly smile at my turning politician at age eighteen. I cannot but help smiling myself...."

Fanny was not amused. Replying by return mail, she upbraided him for spiritual backsliding and warned of the abundant dangers she saw in his situation. Authorship, she predicted, would never bring him fame or fortune. Instead, writers "generally starve to death in some garret or place that no one inhabits so you see what fortune and luck belongs to you if you are one of them class of people!" And even should his writing bring him worldly success, it could well corrupt his immortal soul. "[Had] you been searching the scripture for truth, and praying for the direction of the holy spirit... your time would have been more wisely spent, and your advance to the heavenly ... more rapid." But now he had "taken the Hydra by the head," she warned, gravely risking both failure in this world and damnation in the next. "Now, beware of its mouth." If Lloyd must "seek the Applause of Mortals," she emphasized, "lose not the favor of God, have an eye single to his glory, and you will not lose your soul." She closed with a manipulative comment that redoubled the impact of her seemingly impossible injunction:

> Now, my dear, I must draw to a close and say that I love you dear as ever, especially since you consider your dear mother and are trying by your good behavior to smooth her path to the grave.

When Lloyd finally visited Fanny in July 1823, she broke down in tears. Illness had left her so terribly disfigured and emaciated that he hardly recognized her. Two months later she died, leaving a son who had failed to secure the benediction that mattered most for his primary goals in life.

In the years ahead Garrison would fill this emotional void with memories that reassured him of Fanny's boundless love for him while acknowledging her intimidating power. Though they had lived together only sporadically, he preferred to remember her as a mother "who cared for me with such passionate regard, who loved me so intensely.... How often did she watch over me—weep over me—pray over me." But he also retained other memories, expressed in a poetic eulogy, of a far more prepossessing and larger-than-life figure. He pictured a "masterpiece of woman kind," majestically tall with

> lips more opulently red than wine
> ...raven locks, hung tastefully inclined—
> And then her eyes! So eloquently bright.
> An eagle would recoil before their light!

Determined more than ever to secure both salvation and worldly fame, his memories of his mother always bespoke her continuing dominion over the emotional textures of his life. "I always feel like a little boy when I think of my mother," he would one day tell his children.

Garrison was hardly unique as he struggled to square sanctification with success. In the early years of the nineteenth century many piously raised young men from New England grew to maturity just when rapid mobility, technological advances, and dizzying geographic expansion were weakening traditional family ties. Coming of age in a society that apparently offered a myriad of choices and few restraints fostered acute preoccupations with self and burning desires for independence and worldly fulfillment. Yet these attitudes conflicted profoundly with the fixed Christian morality in which they had been raised, one which stressed upholding high principles and rejecting worldly desires. For many, the ministry offered a vocation that seemed to reconcile these conflicting concerns. During the 1820s young men enrolled in seminaries in unprecedented numbers, causing admission standards to relax and the ministry itself to begin losing its traditionally elite status. Garrison, however, had discovered in journalism a profession that was, instead, rapidly gaining in public esteem as mass politics and an increasingly complex economy led people to sense a heightened need to understand affairs beyond the local community. Ministers projected moral influence, but journalists could exercise power.

As a political writer Garrison now set out to achieve what his mother had prophesied to be impossible. He would gain "the Applause of Mortals" by standing as an unbending foe of the same worldly values he both desired and despised. By denouncing the "licentiousness" of American politics he would also give voice to his hatred of "unregulated passions," the destructive human frailties that had overwhelmed his family. His approach to politics would be militantly antipolitical, placing fixed principles over partisan loyalty. Garrison would develop a deep hostility to any form of compromise and a quickness to regard opponents as immoral personal enemies. In the uncertain and intensely competitive "marketplace of ideas" he would present himself to the reading public as the stern but disinterested servant of his own sense of righteousness. It was an approach that could, of course, only prompt opposition, unpopularity, and failure. Every criticism, in turn, only drove him all the more to seek vindication with harsher statements of denunciation, for to fail, as Fanny Garrison had harshly warned, was "to starve to death in some garret" and to "lose the favor of God."

The 1824 presidential election gave Garrison his first significant opportunity to put his politics before the public. Partisan feelings ran high among Newburyport's "High Federalists," who hated John Quincy Adams nearly as much as his leading opponent, Andrew Jackson, and hoped to subvert his candidacy by supporting the little known Georgian, William Crawford, a politician who had little in common with either Jackson or Adams. Garrison published a series of editorials entitled "The Crisis," in which he excoriated Adams as a pampered aristocrat and a "rank apostate" from high Federalism whose sordid political compromises "need no labored philippic of mine to stamp them with disgrace." Jackson he charged with a "savage and domineering spirit" against whom Garrison felt compelled to arouse the opposition of one and all: "A love of country compels me to warn of a delusion that leads to *slavery*; and I do it at this time juncture because it has taken a deep and amazing hold on [the people]." He also called Jackson to personal account for serious derelictions of duty and gross moral lapses: "As a Christian, sir, as a patriot, as an upright man, you owe it to yourself, your country and your admirers to publicly recant. . .and ask the forgiveness of an injured people." Throughout the campaign he put himself before his readers as a high-minded and wholly disinterested opponent of worldliness, vice, and corruption whose devotion to highest duty required his denunciations. "I have spoken fearlessly and candidly," he assured his readers, "without malice or hoarded animosity." Adams won, and Crawford finished next to last in the election.

Several months after Adams's victory, Garrison's seven-year obligation to Allen's *Herald* ended. As a final gesture before beginning the independent career he had so long anticipated, he indulged himself in two ways, each expressing his conflicting desires for purity and fame. The first was his decision to commission a portrait of himself, an unapologetically vain and worldly gesture that Fanny Garrison would have deplored. Yet the painting's treatment of its subject balanced tellingly against its cost by attempting to convey the image of a deeply preoccupied young man, well dressed yet taking with utter seriousness his own pious thoughts and feelings. Garrison's second gesture to his rite of passage was a poem of eight stanzas which he composed about himself. Revealingly, he titled it "Spirit of Independence" and published it in the *Herald*, his formal introduction to the reading public as a now fully recognized political writer.

> Spirit of Independence! where art thou?—
> I see thy glorious form—and eagle eye,
> Beaming beneath thy mind and open brow—

Thy step of majesty, and proud look high:
Thee I invoke!—O to this bosom fly;
Nor wealth shall awe my soul, nor might, nor power;
And should thy whelps assail,—lank poverty!
or threatening clouds of dark oppression lower,—
Yet these combined—defied! shall never make thee cower!

As the historian R. Jackson Wilson has cogently observed, however, this invocation of the "Spirit of Independence" was more a cry for help than it was a confident statement about the future. "Wealth," "might," and "power" he most certainly wanted, yet he pleaded for protection that they might not "awe my soul." For most of his life, he had been "assail[ed]" by the "whelps...of lank poverty" and "threatening clouds of dark oppression," and their return would signal a crushing defeat. All these dangers, "combined," must always be "defied!" for in the absence of defiance his only recourse would be to "cower." In the years ahead, few would match Garrison's capacity for "defiance," or his self-proclaimed devotion, whatever the cost, to the "Spirit of Independence."

CHAPTER THREE

Independence

In the spring of 1826 Garrison bought a newspaper of his own, thanks to a loan from his former master, Ephriam Allen, whose generous act created a competitor for his own newspaper. Newburyport, however, with 7,000 inhabitants was barely large enough to sustain two papers, and most readers were well-accustomed to Allen's *Herald*. Nevertheless, Garrison purchased the *Essex Courant*, founded two years before by Democratic-Republicans to oppose the Federalists, and promptly disappointed many of his subscribers by turning it, like the *Herald*, into a Federalist sheet. He changed the masthead to read *The Newburyport Free Press* and above it he placed the slogan of high Federalism: "Our Country, Our Whole Country and Nothing But Our Country."

Garrison's inaugural statement repeated the sentiments of his post-apprentice poem, promising that his newspaper's "political course would be in the widest sense of the term, *independent*... subservient to no party, and neither the craven fear of loss, nor threats of the disappointed, nor the influences of power shall ever awe one single opinion into silence." As if to prove this sweeping vow, he revived in the same issue the long standing high Federalist contention that the federal government had given glaring insult to Massachusetts by refusing to compensate the state's expenditures for fighting in the War of 1812. Ten subscribers quit immediately and others soon followed. "We assure those patriotic gentlemen that we erase their names with the same pleasure that we insert MORE THAN THE SAME NUMBER,"

Garrison retorted as subscriptions continued falling. "We *beg* no man's patronage." Thus did Garrison present himself from the first as a righteously independent political writer, standing on principle no matter what the public reaction. "Personal or political offenses we shall try to avoid—the truth, *never*." Controversy, he hoped, would sell his newspapers and broadcast his standing as a serious Christian moralist.

The plain fact was, however, that the Federalist party had long since become moribund. In Massachusetts, politics during the later 1820s now featured complicated factional contests between supporters and opponents of Andrew Jackson, and newsmen who were truly successful had adjusted their stances accordingly. Yet Garrison's antique doctrines gave him personal confirmation that politics should conform above all to Christian values, and supplied a rich vocabulary for denouncing the worldliness he so distrusted in public life. In editorials he consistently embellished political axioms learned during his apprenticeship, insisting that government was being overtaken by turbulent, conspiring factionalists, men driven by a lust for money and immoral influence. Restoring moral order required action by bold leaders who stood aloof from the fray, men like Harrison Gray Otis and Daniel Webster, who set an example through the independent exercise of character and eloquence.

In one important respect, Garrison's political instincts were well grounded. Politics in the 1820s was, in fact, breeding a new secularism that many pious New Englanders besides himself found disturbing. The United States was entering a period of unparalleled economic growth and social dislocation. Powerful networks of commerce, transportation, and communication reinforced regional interdependence and market expansion. Northern cities were growing at rapid rates, as was impoverishment, crime, and a medley of social conflicts. Politicians had begun organizing party machinery that spoke to those new developments and to the common man's mundane preferences. Many conservative spokesmen besides Garrison now warned darkly of the nation's growing infidelity, fueled by unscrupulous demagogues and "wire-workers" who duped the voters with alcohol, flattery, and lies.

As Garrison launched the *Free Press*, a circle of religion-inspired New Englanders were already beginning to mount an impressive counterattack against this wave of "immorality," broadcasting appeals to the public conscience by using the same tools as the politicians—the mass meeting, the printing press, and the efficiently managed voluntary organization. Seeking to revitalize American religious life and moral values, they sponsored powerful evangelists, like Lyman Beecher and Charles G. Finney, and supported religious revivals in the Northeast and throughout the nation. Regardless of his independent posture and primary political interests, Garrison's deep religious values gave him much in common with this growing Protestant crusade. Soon his *Free Press* editorials began denouncing sabbath breakers, tipplers, traffickers in prostitution, dualists, and theatregoers as well as discussing political candidates and issues. Garrison's clear tendency to resistance and denunciation was now being stimulated and expanded by disruptive trends in the larger society itself.

On July 4, 1826, the fiftieth anniversary of the signing of the Declaration of Independence, John Adams and Thomas Jefferson died, and citizens everywhere joined in mourning, whatever their political persuasions. Allen published a eulogy in the *Herald* which, to his surprise, Garrison then excoriated in the *Free Press* for hypocrisy. Allen for years had deplored Jefferson as the "Great Llama of Infidelity," Garrison wrote, and "no greater prostitution of the language" was possible than his sudden and unscrupulous reversal of opinion. Why Garrison chose to turn so vehemently on his generous former patron is not clear. But Allen, hurt, furious, and knowing just how to wound Garrison most deeply, replied by twitting him for his youth, naivete, and inexperience, touching his adversary to the quick by casting aspersions on his most sensitive concern, his public standing. Responding with great asperity, Garrison haughtily dismissed Allen as an unworthy antagonist. "Here, the victory would not be worth the condescension," he remarked, as he publicly denied all debts of loyalty to the one who had assisted him most of all in establishing his career.

But in promoting this quarrel with Allen, Garrison revealed to everyone that his denunciating style of politics now far exceeded any ordinary misgivings about Jeffersonian "infidelity," even in conservative Newburyport. Readers resented his unwarranted attack on the much-respected Allen and grew weary of Garrison's combative tone. All summer, subscriptions fell off. By September the *Free Press* was up for sale, and by December Garrison had his eye set on Boston, ready to sever forever his ties with the place and the people that could most recall his beginnings.

Garrison's efforts to lead the citizens of Newburyport to a purer level of political morality had failed. He had hoped to command his readers' attention, respect, and support by publishing the promptings of conscience and publicly demonstrating his spiritual purity. Instead he had bankrupted his prospects, but Garrison was wholly unable to recognize his loss of the *Free Press* as the public chastisement it plainly was. In his parting statement to his readers, he gave an account of his editorship that allowed him not only to uphold his public dignity, but also to reinterpret his failure as the prelude to still more significant accomplishments. Unable to admit publicly that his readers had deserted him, he claimed instead that "if many have discontinued, many more have taken their places." He was actually resigning, he wrote, "not because my high expectations had not been realized, but for other inducements." Though he actually had no idea of what "inducement" or position he might find next, he had, understandably, to maintain appearances at all cost, for his reputation among those who had known him all his life was far too precious to him to allow any other explanation, either to himself or to the public. Such were the paradoxes of his fierce "independence," connected as it was to his deep sensitivity to society's regard for his character. But far more important, Garrison now interpreted his editorial failure not only as a conventional success, but also as leading him to a higher calling.

In this "time-serving age," Garrison asserted that a publicist such as he who "attempted to walk uprightly or speak honestly cannot rationally calculate upon speedy wealth or preferment." His success, he now decided, should no longer be judged by ordinary standards of income or status. Since his ordinary readers "had rather be flattered than reproved," a morally independent journalist must measure his achievements not by the size of his readership, but by the virulence of his opponents. When others had accused him of "arrogance and unchastened zeal, of malice and envy," it had been, he explained, because of his unbending devotion to truth as an editor who "lashes public follies and vices, who strips deception from its borrowed garb and aims his shafts at corruption." Garrison, by failing, was now growing eager to court public rejection, spurn the ordinary trappings of success, and pursue a far more taxing calling. If he could truly give full voice to his reflexive hatred of the hypocrisy and worldliness he sensed growing around him and actually lead in its downfall, fame and vindication in the long run would be his. The most honorable cause of all could be found in working for society's moral revitalization by presenting it with challenges of unbending truth.

Reflected in Garrison's misrepresentation, excuses, and deeper contemplation on his failure were the first yearnings of a religious visionary who would soon, as an abolitionist, begin prophesying a new and sanctified social order. No longer could he be content to harangue the local Federalists to restore political virtue by returning to "first principles" at the ballot box. Instead, his mission as a publicist would be to reawaken his readers' consciences with the hope of leading them to spiritual purification. To this end, Garrison looked to Boston as the ideal place to start, alive as it was with religious reformers who sought similar goals by forming societies, holding meetings, and publishing newspapers. He arrived in the city in December 1826, prepared to search for a position that might satisfy his expanding aspirations, his quest for success as a self-made man.

Garrison immediately plunged into Boston's rich culture of pious activism. He moved in with Reverend William Collier, a Baptist city missionary who also edited a temperance journal, the *National Philanthropist*. Collier's quarters were a gathering spot for evangelical preachers, visiting missionaries, and a variety of moral reformers, and Garrison absorbed their opinions eagerly. Pushing beyond the sectarian boundaries of his strict Baptist upbringing, he also regularly listened to the evangelical preaching of the powerful Presbyterian revivalist Lyman Beecher, and followed carefully his doctrinal controversies with other Boston divines. Beecher propounded the doctrine of "free agency," which defined sin as willful selfishness. Humanity, however, possessed full freedom to overcome it by accepting Christ. This creed drove the engines of revivalism, supplied theological bedrock for every evangelical reform movement, and moved Garrison away from his mother's sectarianism even as it reinforced those very dogmas with which Garrison had been raised. "As a divine, Lyman Beecher has no equal!" Garrison decided. He also tried mixing in Boston politics, interrupting a party caucus in the Exchange Coffee House to nominate (without prior notice) his hero Harrison Gray Otis for the United States Senate. Soon after, the *Boston Courier* published a letter from a miffed delegate who wanted the name of the disruptive young intruder. In a published reply, Garrison gave voice to his expanding sense of mission and his anxiousness to assert his public presence. "Let me assure him," Garrison emphasized, "that if my life be spared, my name will one day be known to the world—at least to the extent that common inquiry shall be unnecessary. This, I know will be deemed excessive vanity—but time will prove it prophetic." Garrison clearly chafed to finally establish himself. He also must have worried greatly about failing again.

His opportunity came when temperance editor William Collier decided to give up on the poorly subscribed *National Philan-*

thropist and sold it to his printer, Nathaniel White. White then promoted Garrison from his position as typesetter to editor, and in January 1828, the newspaper first appeared under the new editor's direction. At this time, the temperance movement was beginning to develop new and quite militant approaches to the problems of alcohol which, of course, evoked deeply troubling memories for Garrison. His ceaseless impulse to denounce licentiousness and his increasingly rarified career expectations seemed to fit him perfectly for an editorship that condemned "ardent spirits."

Garrison, in fact, was present at the inception of a crusade which would periodically disrupt American politics for over a century. Before the 1820s, American reformers had combatted the problem of alcohol by counseling moderation, regarding strong drink as a health-giving substance when consumed in smaller amounts. By mid-decade, however, newspapers such as the *National Philanthropist* had begun demanding total abstinence, with editor Collier among the first in the nation to issue this stringent demand. Garrison wholeheartedly agreed with the *National Philanthropist*'s pledge to devote its attention "to a suppression of intemperance and its kindred vices, and to the promotion of industry, education and morality." Its motto, as novel as it was controversial, proclaimed that "MODERATE DRINKING IS THE DOWNHILL ROAD TO INTEMPERANCE AND DRUNKENNESS."

Historians have demonstrated that temperance gained much of its support from ambitious promoters of economic development in a Yankee society rapidly moving into industrialization. These men attributed their prosperity to their own self-control and sobriety and believed that stringent abstinence, resulting in a clear-eyed work force and sober body politic, could enable national as well as individual progress. Joining them were evangelical clergy like Lyman Beecher who feared for the nation's moral integrity, churchgoing women who could now oppose drunken male abusiveness, and struggling free blacks for whom temperance promised community pride and the preservation of meager incomes. As Garrison commenced his new editorship these temperance advocates had begun joining to warn the nation that even the mere presence of alcohol, not just its consumption, both spawned and magnified the nation's most terrible vices—particularly gambling, prostitution, rioting, duelling, atheism, desertion, and violent crime. These, in turn, destroyed families, tainted politicians, undermined religion, and stifled all progress.

To overthrow this corruption, reformers followed the theology of "free agency" and called for the moral perfection of each individual through strictures that appealed to conscience. Such regeneration, of course, could only arise in response to warnings from those already saved—morally liberated and courageous prophets like William Lloyd Garrison, who wrote in an early issue of his *National Philanthropist* that his overriding purpose was to "sound the alarm over a slumbering land." Otherwise "the tide of dissolution will continue to swell until neither ark or mountain will be able to save us from destruction." He had now found a cause for which he seemed ideally suited. He had also joined a movement that strongly prefigured the crusade to abolish slavery, the cause in which he would soon play so important a part. The two crusades, temperance and abolitionism, arose from the same social settings, shared the same constituencies, and displayed strikingly similar approaches. Both would demand wholehearted repentance and the immediate cessation of sinful behavior. Both sought their goals by a righteous appeal to conscience issued by inspired moral prophets, and both regarded their leading opponents as willfully godless conspirators. Each group, finally, regarded the sin with which it was struggling as the primal source of all other moral evils besetting the nation. Temperance would shape Garrison's future career as an abolitionist.

Garrison was also moving rapidly away from political journalism. Finally he could hope to present himself to a broadly dispersed but presumably sympathetic readership, not the quarrelsome small-town subscribers that had refused to sustain him in Newburyport. Moreover, he could now treat reform as superior to politics in securing social betterment since moral revolution was now the vital prerequisite for creating Christian government. No longer would he face the humiliation of supporting morally superior but politically unelectable candidates like William Crawford and Harrison Gray Otis. But most important, temperance offered Garrison limitless opportunity to express his hatred of sinful passion, act as an uncompromising moral censor, and anticipate the approval that would surely be his when the moral revolution he had prophesied was finally accomplished. It is hardly surprising that Garrison, after ultimately embracing militant abolitionism, would remain a fervent apostle of temperance throughout his life.

His editorship, however, proved far too zealous to attract enough readers to the *National Philanthropist* to remunerate its owner. In those earliest years, militant temperance provoked more skepticism and jeering dismissal than it would just a decade later. But Garrison, of course, pursued the cause with all the conviction his righteousness could impart, urging that all drinkers be dismissed from their jobs, that intoxicants be prohibited by law, particularly (and tellingly) on ships, that Christian voters support only those candidates who had sworn to abstain completely, and that churches comply by substituting pure grape juice for sacramental wine. Housewives must refuse to offer social drinks to callers, Garrison declared, recognizing "the immense influence which the females of our country are capable of exercising over the manners of the people" and their rapidly growing importance for every evangelical reform.

As Garrison amplified these controversial opinions, he revealed an increasingly comprehensive view of the goals of moral reform. Alcohol, he assured, was not a single or self-contained evil. In addition it constituted the basic source of corruption from which issued a frightening stream of closely related sins, and thus combatting intemperance required denouncing those other forms of corruption as well. Garrison began conceiving of his role as that of a "universal reformer" who must set himself against "evil" whenever he sensed its presence; the formulation fit perfectly his heightening self-awareness as moral prophet who measured his value by the fury of his opponents. He vehemently denounced Sunday mail deliveries as Sabbath-breaking, censured Lord Byron's "unholy profusions of lewdness and impertinence," decried lotteries, and condemned young men who dressed like "profligate coxcombs and disappointed dandies." Going further still, he condemned warfare as un-Christian, endorsed the views of William Ladd, the pioneer American pacifist whom he had first met in Newburyport, and denounced a South Carolina law that forbade the instruction of blacks in reading and writing. As a "universal reformer" primarily committed to crushing intemperance, he now could envision a sweeping Christian regeneration of all of American life. Wholly disinterested in piecemeal improvement, he now anticipated leading the nation toward total redemption, though this would require great sacrifices and bring scorn and abuse that only those possessing great integrity could surmount. In the end, moral revolution would surely come, saving the souls of countless sinners, confirming his foresight and securing his vindication: "I speak in the spirit of prophecy a flashing eye and glow of the heart," he lectured a doubter in 1828. "*The task may be yours to write my biography.*" But just as in Newburyport and just as quickly, many of Garrison's readers grew dissatisfied with his zealotry. By August 1828 the paper had a new editor, and Garrison had still failed to sustain a position for more than six months. Though he masked his reversal with ambiguous statements, he was again stalled, frustrated, and penniless. However, a chance meeting with an unassuming Quaker, Benjamin Lundy, gave him reasons for persisting so compelling that they changed his life.

During the 1820s Lundy was the nation's foremost opponent of slavery, publishing a newspaper titled *The Genius of Universal Emancipation.* As Lundy moved around the upper South, he advocated gradual emancipation and voluntary colonization of blacks. Upon first meeting Lundy in March 1828 at Collier's house, Garrison found himself encountering "one of those rare spirits that rise up in the lapse of many centuries," and he was so deeply moved by Lundy's characterizations of slavery that he dated his conversion to abolitionism from that moment. "I feel I owe everything," he wrote, "instrumentally and under God to Benjamin Lundy." Garrison never did explain exactly why he responded so irrevocably to Lundy's appeals. Although his mother had once spoken highly of blacks, and although Federalists' suspicions of slavery had been strong in New England, he had previously displayed little concern over the plight of African Americans. He seems, moreover, to have had no contract whatsoever with New England's highly activist free black community. Instead, it seems evident that through temperance he discovered that vast new networks of sin would also have to be dismantled in the pending moral revolution. Next, Lundy led him to realize, as would so many other abolitionists, that the sins of slaveowning exemplified more powerfully than anything else the pervasive licentiousness and spiritual bankruptcy he so hated and so roundly denounced.

To the religious reformers, all sins enslaved the souls of those they corrupted. But the slaveholders' conscious decision to seize and physically possess another human being suddenly appeared as inestimably more personal, tangible, and dramatic an act of blasphemy even than was intemperance, for enslavement constituted a direct and calculated usurpation of the power of God himself. It was, above all, God's prerogative alone to rule over all human beings, whatever their race or condition. If intemperance was an act of self-pollution, with grievous consequences for others, enslavement required not only the desecration of one's self, but also the immediate and lifelong degradation of another of God's human creations, equal in His sight to all others.

In other respects, too, slavery stood in sharp contrast to the most cherished of Garrison's own compelling motivations. Long before, he had developed a driving need to assert his spiritual and social independence; slavery, by contrast, seemed to rest entirely on the master's complete domination and the slaves' utter submission. Garrison, since childhood, had despised the destructiveness of unregulated passion; slavery seemed to give masters limitless warrant to vent on their slaves their fullest measure of greed, lust, anger, and irreligion. Garrison, at twenty-three, was locked in an agonizing struggle to secure his contradictory goals of spiritual purity and worldly acclaim. Now he discovered that slavery wrought desecration on the religion of free agency while denying completely the self-help maxims of Benjamin Franklin. Modern scholarly biographers reveal that many abolitionists grew up in healthy family situations that nurtured their commitments to reform. Garrison's abolitionism, by contrast, plainly arose from the trauma and instability of his childhood.

For Garrison, clearly, the slaves' emancipation and his own were now becoming deeply intertwined. His understanding of his own destiny was becoming powerfully attached to that of an oppressed, despised people whom he had never seen and about whom he knew almost nothing. To date, his role had been one of defiant condemnation of the sins of his white New England peers, but by embracing abolitionism he added to his denunciation a sweeping humanitarianism that was truly radical. He now identified with the condition of impoverished and enslaved blacks. No less radical and egalitarian was his daily exhortation that slaves and masters, blacks and whites reassemble their relationship on the basis of Christian justice and brotherhood. Emancipation, for Garrison, promised the redemption of all humanity, the moral revolution that would open a purer phase of history where God's will would prevail. He knew too that a crusade against slavery would surely bring him society's scorn and its most virulent opposition, confirming once and for all his pious tenacity in defense of higher principles. When moral revolution finally arrived with the freeing of those millions of slaves, the ultimate vindication would incontestably be his.

Eager to begin his new crusade, Garrison accepted the first available editorship which opened in late 1828 at Burlington, Vermont's *Journal of the Times*. It had been founded to boost John Quincy Adams's prospects in the 1828 presidential election, but it was clear well before Garrison took up the post that Andrew Jackson would win. Garrison, who despised Adams anyway, felt free to demonstrate his new-found convictions as a budding abolitionist by announcing his leading objectives: crushing slavery, intemperance, and warfare. After dismissing Jackson as "a man whose hands are crimsoned with human innocent blood, whose lips are full of profanity . . . a buyer and seller of human flesh—a military despot," he turned most of his editorial attention elsewhere.

Garrison commented extensively on debate in England's Parliament on West Indian emancipation and hailed the English abolitionists for forming one united society to secure freedom for blacks throughout the British Empire. Americans, Garrison affirmed, ought to emulate this example. The *Journal of the Times* also sponsored a campaign to petition Congress for the abolition of slavery in the District of Columbia. Garrison composed the petition, sent it to postmasters across Vermont, and labored hard to secure the 2,352 signatures that accompanied it to the House of Representatives. There it was tabled, with the concurrence of three New England congressmen. In condemning this "apostasy" Garrison gave his readers full exposure to his abolitionist vehemence and his new-found religious egalitarianism:

Are we—in the Fifty Third Year of the Independence of the United States—are we to gravely discuss the question, whether all men are born free and equal as if it were a new doctrine? Are we to learn, whether the colored of our race are really brutes or human beings? Whether they have bodies capable of suffering, or souls which can never die? Whether it is consistent with the principles of our government to shackle some of our species with galling chains, and to mar their image by applying the whip and the brand? Or whether it is criminal to traffic in human flesh, or degrading to buy and sell in a national capacity?

Responses to Garrison's harshly discordant voice were quick and predictable. The New York *Journal of Commerce* castigated him for intemperate language, while local critics branded him

"Lloyd Garrulous," a "Boston dandy" and a "great egotist who, when talking of himself, displays the pert loquacity of a blue-jay." Responding as usual that he feared far more the "terrible judgments of an incensed God" than the opinions of "timid, half-minded...editors," Garrison stood his ground. After the election was decided, still another of his newspapers slid into bankruptcy.

On March 27, 1829, Garrison published yet another farewell to his readers. But this valedictory, unlike the others, made no rationalization for failure. Instead, Garrison made his abolitionist commitments absolutely clear. Slavery, he wrote, involved "interests of greater moment to our welfare as a republic" than any question since the founding of the nation. Though many were voicing concern over the position of the "miserable Africans," no one had yet undertaken "vigorous and successful measures" to completely "overthrow this fabric of oppression." He trusted in God, he wrote, that "he may be the humble instrument of breaking at least one chain, and restoring one captive to liberty: it will amply repay a lifetime of severe toil."

By April, Garrison was again in Collier's boarding house in Boston where Benjamin Lundy awaited him. Lundy had offered him a co-editor's position with the *Genius of Universal Emancipation*, and Garrison had gladly agreed. Nearly as important, the American Colonization Society had invited him to give a major address at the Park Street Church on the "Dangers to the Nation." Finding himself "somewhat in a hobble from a pecuniary point of view," Garrison had to borrow eight dollars to pay off debts and meet his expenses. And while he looked for temporary work to tide him over until his collaboration with Lundy began, his "very knees knock[ed] together at the thought of speaking before such a large [audience]." Though nearly penniless and for the moment somewhat intimidated, Garrison had found his calling.

CHAPTER FOUR

Emancipation

The American Colonization Society, sponsor of Garrison's address, evolved from a history that illustrated the overwhelming obstacles facing any serious abolitionist. During the American Revolution, antislavery feelings had multiplied, stimulating voluntary emancipations all over the South and emancipation under law in the North. As early as 1790, however, opposition to slavery had begun to recede. Seeking national unity, the original framers of the federal Constitution incorporated formidable protections for the South's planter classes into that document by guaranteeing federal suppression of slave insurrections and by counting the slave population at a three-fifths ratio for purposes of taxation and representation in the House of Representatives. With slavery thus firmly guaranteed by law, the institution gained further strength from hardening racist attitudes and from potent economic expansion. By the time the American Colonization Society was founded in 1816, Eli Whitney's cotton gin had opened countless new opportunities for the South's planters, and serious antislavery feeling had all but expired. Only Benjamin Lundy and a handful of Quaker associates in the upper South continued to oppose the existence of the institution. In this setting, the American Colonization Society began to work to attract supporters.

The Society proposed to resettle American blacks in Africa and encouraged voluntary emancipation, thereby hoping to ameliorate slavery without creating a large and presumably unassimilable free black population. The idea was wildly impractical, a financial and logistical impossibility which blacks spurned as a racist conspiracy. But despite these obstacles the Society reached a peak of popularity in the 1820s, receiving endorsements from eminent clerics and such nationally prominent politicians as Henry Clay, James Monroe, and John Marshall, leaders who saw themselves as judicious humanitarians in their approaches to the problem of slavery. The Society also served as a critical transition point for many soon-to-be abolitionists such as Garrison. To the slaves it promised to bring Christian uplift, supplied by pious masters who had been converted to the cause by benevolent colonizationists. The Society's publication also acquainted emerging abolitionists with the cruelties of slavery and the nationwide oppression awaiting blacks who did become free. In this light, colonization offered the comforting impression that slavery could be ameliorated without serious social disruption, but also provided essential education for people destined to hold far more radical views. Garrison was far along in just such a transition as he stood to deliver his address in the Park Street Church. Technically, he spoke as a colonizationist. In actuality he was becoming a very impatient abolitionist.

While slavery could not be overthrown in an instant, the process must be started at once, Garrison declared. And if people believed "that slavery can be abolished without a struggle with the worst passions of human nature," they were deluding themselves, for prejudice against African Americans ran deep throughout the nation and "bristle[d] like so many bayonets around the slaves." Garrison professed to be "ashamed of my country, . . . sick of our hypocritical cant about the inalienable rights of man," for even as Americans praised the Declaration of Independence they flouted its spirit by silently abetting a system of "barbarity and despotism." "Suppose," he challenged, "the slaves should suddenly become white. Would you shut your eyes upon their sufferings and calmly talk about constitutional limitations? No; you would peal in the ears of task masters like deep thunder." And were such "thundering" to inflame division between North and South, "the fault is not ours if a separation eventually takes place," Garrison stated. This was hardly the moderate viewpoint that colonizationists would find congenial.

Garrison also proposed a sweeping set of actions that undermined colonizationism at its very core, because instead of supporting step-by-step amelioration, he called for a moral revolution. All truly Christian citizens were to join him in a holy crusade, assembling under a banner that proclaimed "Thus saith the Lord God of the Africans: Let this people go that they may serve me," for "we are all alike guilty." Since "slavery is strictly a national sin" in Garrison's view, churches everywhere must "shake off their slumber, combine their energies" and "pour out supplication to heaven on behalf of the slaves." The pious women of New England who "outstrip us" in every reform project must form "charitable associations to relieve the degraded of their sex." Bible-inspired editors must "sound the trumpet of alarm. . . . One press may ignite twenty." Antislavery societies must be formed all over New England to press forward the revolution of public opinion, demanding first freedom for slaves in the District of Columbia and then throughout the country.

Garrison had now issued an unprecedented challenge to several of the major social groups that would, soon enough, supply the leadership of New England's war against slavery—evangelical clerics, reform-minded editors, and pious activist women. He had also outlined the ambitious strategy that would soon drive that war forward—the multiplying of diverse antislavery societies all across the North. Finally, he had articulated perfectly the prophetic spiritual urgency and deep personal engagement that would always inspire that war:

This, sirs, is a cause that would be dishonored and betrayed if I contented myself with appealing only to the understanding. It is too cold, and its processes are too slow for the occasion. I desire to thank God that, since he has given me an intellect so fallible, he has impressed upon me an instinct that is sure. On a question of shame and honor—liberty and oppression—reasoning is sometimes useless, and worse. I feel the decision in my pulse; if it throws no light upon the brain, it kindles a fire in the heart . . .

By rejecting the restraints of "half way" colonizationism, Garrison had discovered in a new cause the outlines of a new religious creed as well, one which promised to liberate and equip him to take God's side as the leading actor in a cosmic drama to redeem a fallen nation while securing his own salvation and achieving his destiny. Ready to make supreme sacrifices and to prove his fitness for his prophetic role, he quickly left Boston for Baltimore and his new collaboration with Benjamin Lundy.

Life in Lundy's boarding house gave Garrison some persuasive new reasons to reject colonization. Free blacks William Watkins and Jacob Greener shared his quarters and told him directly why they so bitterly rejected the Society's methods and goals. This was Garrison's first experience in living with African Americans, vastly different associates than the aggressively pious Boston reformers. Garrison also got a full exposure to the intense but unpretentious spirituality of Lundy and his fellow Quakers, only confirming all the more that his new religion had placed him in a community of like-minded saints.

Garrison's collaboration with Lundy was also a surprisingly congenial one, even though his condemnatory style contrasted sharply with his co-editor's patient approaches. On the deepest level both agreed fully as to slavery's terrible sinfulness. Since both were experienced editors and wanted to keep their public positions clear to their readers, Lundy and Garrison agreed that each should initial his own articles. Lundy characteristically presented a series of essays praising Haiti as a refuge for emancipated slaves. Garrison, by contrast, cast aside any remaining belief in gradual emancipation to declare himself an "immediate abolitionist," demanding that those who "traffick in human flesh" repent at once because "the slaves are entitled to immediate and complete emancipation." Lundy's complete willingness to give his young colleague free editorial rein allowed Garrison to state his opinions as forcefully as possible.

Immediatism was not a doctrine original to Garrison, but few before him had espoused it, and fewer still with his vehemence. Yet his was certainly a logical response to the manifest failure of gradual emancipation, for as Garrison knew well, slaveholders had shown no sympathy for moderate schemes. Garrison appreciated, moreover, that abolitionism was making renewed progress in England since activists there had ceased supporting the moral arguments for gradual or compensated emancipation and adopted the immediatist principle. His growing fear of possible slave insurrections seemed to add still more truth to the necessity of immediatism. In late 1829, an inspired black artisan from Boston, David Walker, issued his famous *Appeal*, calling on slaves to take their freedom, by force if necessary. Garrison praised Walker's "impassioned and determined spirit" while condemning his call for violence; he proposed instead to his readers with immediatist logic that "if we liberate the slaves, and treat them as brothers and men, shall we not take away all motives for rebellion?" Undergirding all these arguments for immediatism was the wellspring of Garrison's newly discovered abolitionist religion. Closely akin to the purifying act of religious conversion, this divine warrant freed and compelled him to strike out at slavery with no remaining reservations. And as he set out to do so in the columns of *The Genius*, he also attempted to unshackle himself from the memories that still bound him to his tragic and unrewarding past.

Baltimore, of course, had been Fanny Garrison's final home and contained for Garrison a wealth of painful associations. Newburyport, too, called forth recollections of his family tragedies, his numerous failures, and personal humiliations. Now once again a resident of Baltimore, he struck out in the fall of 1829 at the memories of his New England upbringing by publishing bitter accusations against a respected Newburyport merchant, Francis Todd, who engaged in the coastal slave trade. Todd had transported roughly eighty slaves from Baltimore to New Orleans, a perfectly legal transaction, but when Garrison heard of it he declared in print that men such as Todd were "enemies of their own species—highway robbers and murderers" who "SHOULD BE SENTENCED TO SOLITARY CONFINEMENT FOR LIFE." He then posted a copy of this bitter attack to his old master, Ephriam Allen, requesting its publication there in the Newburyport *Herald*. Garrison clearly wanted to demonstrate to all who remembered him that his unshakable devotion to conscience had now led him to command the highest of all moral ground, and that he was perfectly justified in returning to visit judgment on one of their leading citizens.

But as it turned out, Garrison, not Todd, received the jail sentence. The state of Maryland sued Garrison for libel on Todd's behalf in January 1830, and the jury found for the plaintiff in the amount of $100.00. Unable to pay the fine, Garrison was remanded to the Baltimore jail while Ephriam Allen, who knew all too well some of his old apprentice's deeper urgings, explained to the citizens of Newburyport that Garrison was too much "prompted by vanity; that a love of display, and an eagerness for notoriety are the main springs of his devotion." *The Genius of Universal Emancipation*, always financially uncertain despite Lundy's dedication, suspended publication as an unrepentant Garrison adjusted to the new but rather pleasant accommodations where a warden gave him considerable freedom to write and to socialize.

For forty-nine days Garrison explored every possibility of personal aggrandizement in his self-proclaimed martyrdom. Eager to call widest attention to his situation and to himself, he printed and distributed widely (with the last of his funds) a pamphlet, *A Brief Sketch of the Trial of William Lloyd Garrison*, that proclaimed his innocence. Fuelling the controversy, he wrote barbed notes to Francis Todd, to the sentencing judge, and to the prosecuting attorney, attempted without success to goad Ephriam Allen into a public dispute over the case, and wrote to inform the citizens of Boston in a letter published in the Boston *Advertiser*. Now without a newspaper or even his personal freedom, Garrison was convinced that he could nevertheless continue to promote his reputation and his cause, assuring one of his confidants that no single event in the struggle against slavery had commanded more attention than his trial and imprisonment. He was fearful, he wrote, that he "was in danger of being lifted up beyond measure, even in prison, by excess panegyric and extraordinary sympathy." That, of course, was exactly what Garrison hoped for.

He also relished every drama that could be extracted from his incarceration. Comparing himself to the imprisoned apostle Paul, he wrote antislavery lectures and letters. He was also allowed to sharply interrogate slaveholders who came to the jail to retrieve runaways. When queried by one of them, "How would you like to have a black man marry your daughter?", Garrison took exquisite delight in pointing out the self-evident responsibility of all planters for siring the racially mixed population already present in the South. Garrison, reported his prison experiences almost euphorically, for what could be a greater badge of purity and distinction than his martyrdom for standing with such solitary courage against the most grievous of all sins? The collapse of his fourth newspaper and his own bankrupted finances bothered him not at all; he now felt more successful than ever, for the religion of abolition assured his liberation from all restraints and doubts. "I pay no rent and am bound to make no repairs—and enjoy all the luxury of independence divested of its cares," he wrote laughingly to a friend. "I strut like the lions of the day, and of course attract a great number of visitors." Indeed, he revealed, "so agreeable is my confinement that I have no occasion to call on my philosophy or my patience."

Stripped for the moment of a job, income, property, family, community ties, and even his physical liberty, Garrison now had only his religious cause, immediate emancipation, to define his identity and set his purpose. His only talents need be those of denunciation, his only strength the daring and truth of his moral vision, and his only claims to the public's attention his sense of unmatched righteousness. Abjah Garrison had liberated himself by deserting his family, Fanny through religion, and James through alcohol. Unlike his parents and brother, however, William Lloyd Garrison's self-emancipation came through an aggressive challenge to society, rather than through withdrawal:

> How do I bear up under my adversities? I answer—like the oak— like the Alps—unshaken, storm-proof. Opposition, and abuse, and slander, and prejudice, and judicial tyranny, are like oil to the flame of my zeal. I am not dismayed; but bolder and more confident than ever. I say to my persecutors,—"I bid you defiance." Let the courts condemn me to fine and imprisonment for denouncing oppression: Am I to be frightened by dungeons and chains? can they humble my spirit? do I not remember that I am an American citizen? and, as a citizen, a freeman, and what is more, a being accountable to God? I will not hold my peace on the subject of African oppression. If need be, who would not die a martyr to such a cause?

That cause also involved him directly in the fates of three million slaves and set him in full confrontation with the nation's most powerful political and economic institutions.

Liberation of a more mundane sort arrived from Arthur Tappan, who paid Garrison's fine. The Tappan brothers, Arthur and Lewis, were the most powerful of New York City's evangelical philanthropists, rich businessmen who underwrote revivalists like Lyman Beecher and financed a myriad of moral reform projects. Both brothers were already growing disillusioned with the American Colonization Society and were taken by Garrison's courageous witnessing for immediate emancipation. Anxious to establish himself with these powerful sympathizers and "heartily sick" of "disorganizing and oppressive" southern "habits, doctrines and practices," Garrison hurried from Baltimore to New York City to follow up on Arthur Tappan's promise of further financial aid. Upon meeting him, the Tappans were impressed by Garrison's "manly form, buoyant spirit and countenance beaming with conscious rectitude," and renewed their promise of assistance in underwriting his effort to start a new abolitionist newspaper. By August 1830, Garrison was resettled in Boston at Collier's boarding house, worrying about a civil suit from the ever-litigious Francis Todd and working up ideas for his next editorial venture.

While pondering his prospects, Garrison took to the lecture circuit against the colonizationists as a spokesman for immediate emancipation. After failing twice to secure the use of a lecture hall in Newburyport, he made his first visit to Philadelphia. There he boarded with James and Lucretia Mott, friends of Benjamin Lundy's and followers of Quaker reformer Elias Hicks, who hated slavery and lived with a studied simplicity. The Motts, like most Hicksite Quakers, viewed all denominational religion with suspicion and rejected all complex theology as dogmatic selfishness. Instead, they strove to emulate Christ's simple and loving example in their daily lives, rejecting all claims of external, worldly authority, human or spiritual. Garrison entered their home a strong sectarian, still clinging to his strict Baptist creeds. He left with a much expanded religious understanding, so impressed was he by "this kind, tolerant catholic spirit" and their fervent embrace of immediate emancipation. Another tie to Garrison's past, the faith nurtured by his mother, was now being severed. Henceforth, he would show an increasing hostility to orthodox Protestantism and institutionalized religion in general, seeking instead the spontaneous inspiration of God's will, the divine impulses of conscience from above. Garrison had also now gained some powerful new supporters to add to the Tappans, and Philadelphia would always contain a busy circle of his followers. Just as important, however, his highly personalized new creed now motivated a much expanded sphere of activity for universal reform and immediate abolitionism.

Shortly thereafter, Boston provided Garrison with even more new converts and still greater reason to distrust Protestant orthodoxy. Since no church would agree to rent him space to deliver an abolitionist lecture, he was forced to hold forth at the local Freethinkers' Society. After he had completed his lecture on October 15, 1830, his hero Lyman Beecher told him straight out that his fanatical views were misguided and dangerous.

From that moment on, Beecher and the Protestant establishment he spoke for were Garrison's idols no longer. Those who did applaud his speech enthusiastically were, revealingly, two reverends that Beecher considered religious infidels, Unitarian clergymen Samuel Sewall and his cousin Samuel J. May. Though leery at first of Garrison's vituperative language, they accepted his doctrines warmly and promised funds for the proposed newspaper.

The impoverished Garrison and the allies he was gathering throughout New England came from quite contrasting origins. May and Sewall, for example, counted among Boston's elite, were Harvard-educated, descended from eminent Puritans, and lived off earnings of prosperous forbears. The Tappan brothers, though of common origins, had achieved great wealth and position on their own. The Motts, while living frugally, were nevertheless involved in a transatlantic community of Quakers in England and the United States that thrived on trade, manufacturing, and the multiplication of investments. All were social rebels, regarding slavery as a force that defied God's law and therefore stifled the moral improvement and material progress that their own lives embodied so convincingly. All of them had also achieved some measure of the power and respectability that Garrison had always coveted. Now, by leading them to immediate emancipation, he had begun securing their acceptance and financial support—all the result of his defiant refusal to compromise. By spurning the lure of worldly corruption, he had now secured the patronage of the wealthy. He accepted this situation gladly, fully satisfied that he had not once sacrificed his principles or jeopardized his "independent" standing as a "self-made" man. And for all of their social differences Garrison and his new associates did indeed share a religious persuasion that overcame class distinctions and began to create a close community of Christian believers. Their shared devotion to evangelicalism and to the promptings of God's voice within consecrated them in the common cause of moral revolution and bound them together spontaneously as the truest Christians of all. Garrison's

religion of abolitionism was slowly beginning to create a dispar-
ate community of closely-knit saints. From it he could draw a
heightened spiritual assurance, especially since so many in that
community seemed to look to him for leadership.

By late December of 1830 Garrison's new friends began anticipating the appearance of his latest newspaper. Assisted by two
additional converts, Stephen S. Foster and Isaac Knapp, Garrison procured type, paper, and access to a press. On Saturday
morning, January 1, 1831, four hundred copies of the *Liberator*
were circulating in Boston, the first fruits of Garrison's fifth attempt to succeed as a journalist. This time, though, his situation
was entirely different, and filled with opportunity and danger.
Before, he had been held to account by an owner or a stub-
bornly partisan political constituency, as when working with
Lundy on the *Genius*, and he had been obliged to share the editorial platform. Now, no overseeing agent of any sort could prevent him from fully expressing himself. During his earlier
editorships he had felt bound by residues of memory from which
he sought release; now, his sense of prophetic leadership in the
religion of abolitionism sharpened his vision of the future and
suppressed the past. Viewed in this fashion, his choice of a title,
the *Liberator*, carried an obvious double meaning. As it called so
resoundingly for freeing the slaves, it also announced the emancipation of its editor. But emancipation was filled with as much
risk as exhilaration. Since he and his newspaper were nearly as
one, should it fail so would he—privately, publicly and
comprehensively—be forfeiting irrevocably his destiny. Little
wonder that he propelled his famous introductory manifesto
with a staccato repetition of the first person singular, demanding above all that the nation must NEVER ignore either his cause
or him:

> I am aware, that many object to the severity of my language, but is
> there not cause for my severity? I *will be* harsh as truth, and as un-
> compromising as justice. On this subject I do not wish to think,
> write or speak with moderation. No! No! Tell a man whose house is

on fire to give a moderate alarm; tell him to moderately rescue his wife from the hands of the ravishers, tell the mother to gradually extricate her babe from the fire to which it has fallen;—but urge me not to use moderation in a cause like the present. I am in earnest—I will not equivocate—I will not excuse—I will not retreat an inch and I WILL BE HEARD.

African Americans, seeking their own liberation, insured that Garrison would not be ignored. After a full year of publication, the *Liberator* counted but fifty white subscribers, but free blacks throughout the North supported the paper impressively. The well-organized African American communities in major urban centers were led by people like the talented and wealthy James Forten of Philadelphia. Forwarding payment for twenty-seven subscriptions, Forten declared himself "much pleased" with the *Liberator*, especially because Garrison's voice of protest had begun to inspire African Americans to speak for themselves. The *Liberator*, Forten wrote, "has roused up the spirit of our young people that had been slumbering for years, and [now] we shall produce writers able to vindicate our cause." Garrison was eager to pay close attention to those loyal supporters, meeting with local black groups in Boston's "Nigger Hill" district and traveling at the invitation of Forten and his son-in-law, Robert Purvis, to address the Philadelphia Free People of Color Association. Admitting freely now that the *Liberator* survived no thanks to whites—"they do not sustain it, it belongs emphatically to the people of color—it is their organ," he sought ways to reciprocate the favor to his new constituency. For the first time he tried to understand and work constructively with the people on whose loyal support he was now truly dependent. If slavery proved impervious to his attacks, he wrote Samuel J. May, at least "I may be able to elevate our free colored population on the scale of society."

Though they shared the experience of poverty, enormous differences of race, culture, and history clearly separated Garrison and his new African American collaborators. Like most white abolitionists, he understood freedom as a moral, universal, religious absolute. African Americans, by contrast, understood freedom as a pragmatic struggle against day-to-day racial discrimination and oppression. Garrison, moreover, shared with most white abolitionists a Protestant zeal for moral homogeneity that left him wholly ill-equipped to tolerate, let alone value, the reality of social and cultural differences between races and classes. Believing always in the regenerative power of conversion, however, it is hardly surprising that Garrison was but the first of many white abolitionists to attempt to make over the lives of African Americans, offering them benevolent guidance in learning the widely held Protestant values of working hard, cultivating piety, and squelching vice. And finally, the feelings of profound guilt that allowed Garrison to project his imagination so empathetically toward unseen slaves on far-removed plantations also spilled over awkwardly into relationships with blacks close to home: "I never rise to address a colored audience," he informed them, "without feeling ashamed of my own color, ashamed of being identified with a race of men who have done you so much injustice." To "make atonement," he explained, "I have solely dedicated my health, and strength and life to your service."

Yet Garrison's relationship with free African Americans during the 1830s also had indisputably positive elements. Northern free black communities already placed their own high premiums on "moral uplift" and drew strong feelings of personal achievement and community pride from their church activities, temperance societies, young men's improvement associations, and Bible groups. From these apparently familiar activities, Garrison and his white colleagues could only believe that their exhortations for uplift were encouraging goals which the black community already endorsed as its own. They called for free African Americans to comport themselves honorably and piously so as to convince whites of their fitness for equality. And though endlessly patronizing, his advice was indeed supportive of values that African Americans themselves prized highly.

But more important than Garrison's advice was his prophetic voice, his success in offering his black readers comprehensive visions of hope and ultimate victory. These he set forth boldly in a decade when racist attitudes and patterns of discrimination were becoming significantly more oppressive, and when a case could be made that prospects for African Americans' freedom were actually diminishing considerably:

> I believe, as firmly as I do my own existence, that the time is not far distant when you and the trampled slaves will all be free—free in the spirit as well as in the letter—and enjoy the same rights in this country as other citizens. Every one of you shall sit under your own vine and fig-tree, and none shall molest or make you afraid.
>
> I lose sight of your present situation, and look at it only in futurity. I imagine myself surrounded by educated men of color, the Websters, and Clays, and Hamiltons, and Dwights, and Edwardses of the day. I listen to their voice as Judges, and Representatives, and Rules of the people—the whole people.
>
> I do not despair of seeing the time when our State and National Assemblies will contain a fair proportion of colored representatives.

As will be discussed, African Americans of that time and historians of times since have found ample reasons to criticize Garrison's patronizing and racial bias. That many blacks also remained his lifelong supporters and subscribers to the *Liberator* is also understandable.

While free blacks were sustaining the *Liberator*, a remarkable slave named Nat Turner made its editor instantly famous. In the summer of 1831, a massive slave rebellion broke out in British Jamaica, increasing the anxieties of southern planters already complaining bitterly about the *Liberator* in general and Garrison's republication of parts of David Walker's *Appeal* in particular. Shortly thereafter, Southampton County Virginia exploded with Turner's bloody insurrection, and by the end of August over sixty whites had been killed. Turner and most of his band were quickly captured and executed, and next followed grim re-

prisals, which included the savage beating, executing, and de-
porting of hundreds of suspected collaborators.

Though an avowed pacifist, Garrison's reaction to Turner's
bloody deeds went beyond easy condemnation to reveal a more
complex attitude. While deploring the slaves' use of violence, he
remarked that "I do not condemn *them* and approve similar conduct in *white* men." "Of all the living," he contended, "our
slaves have the best reason to assert their rights by violent measures, inasmuch as they are more oppressed than others." So
while upholding the highest standards of nonviolence, Garrison's abhorrence of the oppression endured by the slaves compelled him to praise their Christian forbearance all the more. He
had to admire and empathize with the reasons for resistance, if
not the violent deeds themselves, done in the name of emancipation.

As news of the rebellion spread, hate mail deluged Garrison's
office, from New Englanders as well as Southerners, charging
him with responsibility for the revolt and in some cases even
threatening death. A North Carolina newspaper recommended
the literal "barbecuing" of abolitionists, and the article was reprinted in the powerful Washington D.C. *National Intelligencer*
which editorialized in the same issue that Garrison in particular
must be stopped. Southern state legislatures passed laws ban-
ning the circulation of the *Liberator*, and Governor James Hamil-
ton and U.S. Senator Robert Y. Hayne of South Carolina
attempted to persuade public officials in Massachusetts to suppress the newspaper. The Georgia legislature drew up a bill offering a fifteen-thousand-dollar reward to the intrepid soul who
would kidnap Garrison and bring him south for trial. From the
standpoint of nearly every southern white, immediate emancipation was, from the first, an idea deserving only of suppression.

In the midst of the tumult Garrison was understandably
elated. "The *Liberator* is causing most extraordinary movement
in the slave states, among the whites" he wrote excitedly to a
friend. "I am constantly receiving anonymous letters, filled

with abominable and bloody sentiments. These trouble me less than the wind," he exulted. "I was never so happy and confident as I am at the present time." Nat Turner had given Garrison a bounty of attention that matched his grandest dreams. The insurrection was making him known throughout the nation, just as he had prophesied six years before. It also seemed to vindicate as only such a catastrophe could his dire prophesies that God would rain condemnation on a sinful nation that refused emancipation.

The *Liberator* was not even remotely the cause of Turner's insurrection. It had no slave-state subscribers and no clandestine network of southern African Americans to spirit copies from reader to reader. But Garrison, like every other enterprising journalist, did exchange his newspaper with well over a hundred editors, many from the South. Outraged by the paper's tone, these southern journalists would quote the *Liberator* extensively while editorializing hotly on abolitionist fiendishness. Northern editors often did likewise, reprinting for their readers noteworthy abolitionist rhetoric and examples of southern editorial outrage. Finally Garrison would reply to these comments, completing the circle of controversy and beginning it anew by publicly excoriating all parties, thus commencing another round of acrimony. In the free marketplace of ideas, Garrison was finally discovering how to sell condemnation to the world. The *Liberator* would never be rich with subscribers, but after only one year Garrison could be satisfied that he was certainly being HEARD by everyone, and even believed by a few.

The next step, Garrison decided, was to organize a movement around his growing public recognition. "You may soon expect to hear of the formation of an antislavery society in the city, its principles as steadfast as the pillars of truth," he informed a Boston confidant. "There are staunch abolitionists here who are ready for action, and whom no danger and scoffs can frighten." Preparations for New England's war against slavery were beginning, and Garrison fully expected to act as its spiritual prophet and commanding general.

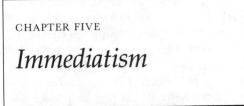

CHAPTER FIVE

Immediatism

The founding of the New England Anti-Slavery Society was laden with inspirational symbolism. Braving a raging snowstorm, thirteen intrepid abolitionists (the same number, they noted, that attended the Last Supper) slogged up "Nigger Hill" on December 6, 1832, to gather in a basement schoolroom of Boston's African Baptist Church. After some debate, those "antislavery apostles," as they came to be known, agreed that all slaves had an indisputable right "to immediate freedom from personal bondage of any kind." Mere "differences of complexion," they further concurred, "were no reason for some people to deprive others of their natural rights, or subject them to disability." Last, the Society's founders set themselves three objectives: peaceful and immediate emancipation, opposition to colonization, and improvement of the lives of African American free people by obtaining "for them equal civil and political rights and privileges with the whites." Arnold Buffum, a Quaker whose strong ties to British abolitionists gave him international credentials, was elected president. The more provincial William Lloyd Garrison, who became the corresponding secretary, attempted to capture the larger meaning of the gathering: "We have met tonight in this obscure schoolhouse, our members are few and our influence limited." But "mark my words," he prophesied, "Faneuil Hall shall ere long echo with the principles we have set forth. We shall shake the nation..." The passage of ten years, he predicted, would witness the end of slavery.

Garrison's position as corresponding secretary gave him a strong influence over the Society while leaving him free to continue to manage the *Liberator*. He also declined to make his paper the Society's official organ, choosing instead to preserve his editorial freedom and to remain independent from any other Society members who might take exception to his vituperation and extreme appeals to principles. Experience had finally taught him well. Never again would Garrison let himself be beholden to others when expressing editorial opinions. Though now a leader of the New England Anti-Slavery Society but with his cherished independence assured, Garrison set about redeeming some of his prophesies by attacking the American Colonization Society.

Garrison's rejection of the Colonization Society was already well-known, but now he held nothing back. Its "motives and controlling incentive," he declared, "may be summed up in a sentence—*they have an antipathy to blacks*." Because of this fatal hatred the Society practiced a bogus and destructive philanthropy, pretending to condemn slavery and work for black uplift, but actually causing the opposite. Its supposedly practical plan for slow but steady emancipation was really nothing but racist equivocation which only strengthened the institution of slavery and degraded African Americans everywhere. The truly practical approach was, of course, immediate emancipation, the wholesale rejection of any compromise. Anything less deflected attention from the nation's fundamental problem—slavery and "colorphobia"—and until whites had accepted blacks as free citizens, digressions on "practical" alternatives to immediatism only reinforced prejudice and complacency. As Garrison liked to comment, the "genius of the abolition movement is to have *no plan*." Though strongly believing that full black equality should be preceded by a careful program of white-sponsored "uplift," the unequivocal demand for immediate emancipation was, to Garrison, a program that always explained itself.

By June 1832, Garrison had finished perusing the American Colonization Society's publications and with funds again from

Arthur Tappan printed up his findings. His *Thoughts on African Colonization* was an unwieldy, two-hundred-and-forty-page compendium composed, in part, of racist statements and avowals of support for slavery from dozens of leading colonizationists. Garrison also included strong words from African American spokesmen, words which demonstrated their unremitting hostility to colonization and firm commitment to achieving emancipation and equality within the United States. To these he added his own editorial commentary as well, proclaiming that colonizationists denied the religious truth that God had created all humans in His image, whatever their race. Colonizationist bigotry was therefore a defiance of Holy Scripture and threatened with damnation all who remained in the Society. They had absolutely no moral foundation by which to justify segregation, to prevent intermarriage, or to allow the toleration of slavery for even a moment. In fact, gradualism of any sort, not just colonization, only perpetuated social chaos and moral degradation, Garrison challenged. Immediate emancipation, by contrast, would open a new and glorious era of Christian reconciliation between the races. Once granted the right to the fruits of their labors, the freed slaves would seek education and religious instruction, turning themselves from potential rebels into pious, trustworthy, productive citizens. Though Garrison stressed that the former slaves "shall not immediately exercise the right of suffrage...or be free of the benevolent restraints of guardianship," he also guaranteed that immediatism would mark the beginning of an instantaneous transformation of human relationships. Instead of being degraded by colonization, liberated African Americans would begin at once working to secure their own "instruction and subsequent admission to all the trusts, offices, honor and enrichments of intelligent freemen."

In challenging the Colonization Society, Garrison assumed a predictably heroic posture, claiming to stand alone against many "formidable opponents," including the "potent engines" of the press, the "powerful influence" of the clergy, and "men of wealth and elevated station." But for once Garrison's *Thoughts*

actually brought him more converts than critics. It was published just as the American Colonization Society began a precipitous decline in the aftermath of Nat Turner's insurrection.
As a consequence of that revolt, many members of the Society
supported in 1832 a gradual emancipation bill debated in the
Virginia legislature by which masters would be compensated
and slaves expelled. When the bill failed, all hopes ended (if
there ever had been any) for a negotiated plan of gradual emancipation, and serious defections from colonization followed.
"Conversions from colonization to abolition principles are rapidly multiplying in every quarter," Garrison noted with excited
pride.

For once he did not exaggerate. *Thoughts on Colonization* sold
nearly 3,000 copies, impressive by standards of the time, and
Arthur Tappan circulated them throughout his wide network of
evangelical co-workers. In Ohio, Theodore Dwight Weld, a student in Cincinnati's Lane Seminary, received a copy and soon
plunged the school into controversy over immediate emancipation. Just outside Cleveland, at Western Reserve College, pro-
fessors Elizur Wright, Jr. and Beriah Green created controversy
as well, and soon they and their followers joined forces with
Weld to create a major center of radical abolitionism. Closer to
New England, a similar pattern developed. William Goodell,
Garrison's successor as editor of the *National Philanthropist*,
renounced colonization for immediatism, as did able Boston
attorneys Ellis Gray Loring and David Lee Child. In Pennsylvania, J. Miller McKim (Garrison's future son-in-law) led a secession from colonizationism, as did Nathaniel P. Rodgers, Parker
Pillsbury, and Stephen S. Foster from New Hampshire. The
New England Anti-Slavery Society's handful of apostles was
starting to grow into a small army of saints. Though Garrison's
warfare with the colonizationists would continue for several
years, victory was almost his even as he opened his campaign.

Exposing the pitfalls of colonization proved much less challenging for Garrison than his pledge to "elevate" his African
American neighbors. Bondage could never be ended, he and his

colleagues reasoned, if bigotry inhibited people from enrolling in their crusade. Hoping to overturn racism with more than just biblical exhortation, abolitionists set about to promote further the educational accomplishments of free African Americans, thereby putting the lie to all claims of their innate inferiority. In Cincinnati, Weld and his fellow seminarians outraged local whites by developing self-help programs in the black community. Soon he and his followers would move on to Oberlin, founding the nation's first venture in racially integrated coeducation. In upstate New York, Beriah Green, fresh from Western Reserve College, took up the presidency of Oneida Institute, a racially mixed manual labor school that was destined to graduate an impressive group of African American leaders. In New Haven, Connecticut, the Reverend Simeon S. Jocelyn, white minister of an African American church, wrote Garrison to seek his assistance in founding an all-black college. Arthur Tappan had already pledged one thousand dollars toward the twenty-thousand-dollar total needed to open Jocelyn's school, with the balance to be raised in equal amounts from African Americans and whites. "The colored people begin to feel their strength and use it," Garrison declared. He praised Jocelyn's "disinterested and unremitting toil" and set forth to assist with planning and fundraising. But in New Haven, where Jocelyn's project quickly "touched the very *quick* of oppression by promising the prospect of equality," its foes united to crush the college before it was even planned. The mayor, aldermen, and seven hundred white citizens met to pass resolutions condemning the all-black college as a threat to domestic order and an insult to nearby Yale.

Garrison was genuinely stunned, surprised, as he wrote that "Christian people in New Haven behave no better than they do in South Carolina" when it came to matters of race. In this regard, the acute observer of America in the 1830s, Alexis de Tocqueville, remarked that "race prejudice seems stronger in the states that have abolished slavery than in those where it still exists, and nowhere is it more intolerant than in the states where it has never been known." Slavery had never become rooted in

Connecticut, but a virulent white supremacy had—not only there, but increasingly throughout much of the North, for as white male political rights and economic choices expanded, prejudice against African Americans also intensified. Garrison and his colleagues were now being forced to learn just how deep and tangled those roots had become.

Soon after their New Haven failure, Garrison and the New England Anti-Slavery Society made another attempt to sponsor African American education in Connecticut. An unusually tenacious Quaker schoolmistress named Prudence Crandall had decided in early 1833 to admit a black child to her private academy for girls in Canterbury. After incensed white parents withdrew their children in response, Crandall agreed with Garrison's suggestion to begin recruiting an all-black student body, assisted by free advertising and warm endorsements published in the *Liberator*. Soon after the entire town erupted in angry opposition. Garrison, as well as Samuel May, Arnold Buffum, and Arthur Tappan flew to Crandall's defense as the townspeople put the school under economic boycott, harassed her and her students, poisoned her well with animal feces, and secured a state law that made operating such a school illegal. By August, Crandall, who had continued to defy the law, had been in and out of jail and was beginning a tempestuous period of litigation, which she finally won. Vindicated by law but discouraged about her school, she chose to marry and ultimately leave Canterbury forever.

The precipitous departure of Prudence Crandall was a particularly stinging rebuff to Garrison, who for several years had been stressing the importance of female influence in forwarding the abolitionist cause. His thinking reflected commonplace assumptions of male evangelicals about gender roles and reform, for Garrison believed that women's auxiliaries would support but remain subordinate to a male-directed movement. Acting accordingly, he had set out to be Crandall's righteous protector, affable confidant, and wise advisor, writing Isaac Knapp that she was a "wonderful woman, as undaunted as if she had the whole world on her side." With gallant gestures and close personal attention, he tried to secure his superior position by winning her trust and affection.

Crandall, however, refused throughout the controversy to let Garrison speak for her or to force her into situations not of her own choosing. When Garrison excoriated her local opponents she quickly told him to stop, since his vehemence only increased the townspeople's anger and her own personal risk. Then Garrison tried to satirize those who charged Crandall with race-mixing by placing a fraudulent "Wife Wanted" advertisement in the *Liberator*. The ad requested information about "any young, respectable intelligent colored woman" who would be willing to risk "insults and reproaches" by "becoming the partner of a white man." Crandall, indignant, demanded that Garrison stop creating indiscretions which embarrassed and undermined her. Their relationship collapsed entirely when Crandall insisted on conducting her own legal defense and writing publicly on her own behalf, rather than relying on direction from Garrison or any other person. Remarking sourly that Crandall now felt herself "exalted above measure," a disillusioned Garrison expressed relief when she finally chose to give up her fight for the less aggressive role of domesticity. Though commenting snidely on Crandall's choice of a husband, he also observed that "she had better take advantage of her marriage and move on with flying colors."

He had attempted to dominate a woman who was every bit the equal of Fanny Garrison in strength of purpose and independence, and in failing, learned lessons that governed his attitudes and behavior toward women from then on. Abolitionism would soon bring forward extraordinary feminists who insisted on power for themselves in the movement and equality for women everywhere. Whenever they made these demands, a deferential Garrison would always be counted in the vanguard of their male supporters. But when he married, he was to choose a spouse who would never think to stand up to him as Prudence Crandall had done.

In March 1833, the *Liberator* announced Garrison's plan to broaden the focus of abolitionism to an international level by making a trip to England. As a special agent of the New England Anti-Slavery Society, his ostensible purpose was to raise funds from British abolitionists to support the establishment of a manual labor school for "colored youth" in the United States. The manual labor approach, common in American colleges and seminaries, allowed students to offset tuition and fees by working on the school farm; it was a way to inculcate steady habits and a love of physical labor while cultivating the intellect. To meet the cost of his trip, Garrison traveled from city to city for six weeks, speaking before groups of free African Americans and collecting their donations. His listeners always received him warmly and gave generously. Garrison, however, was incapable of accepting their trust and support on its own terms, so preoccupied was he with his own dramatic role as foremost liberator of the oppressed:

> The highest interest and most intense feelings were felt and exhibited by the audience. They wept freely—they clustered around me in throngs, each one eager to receive the pressure of my hand and implore Heaven's choicest blessings upon my head. You cannot imagine the scene, and my pen is wholly inadequate to describe it. As I stood before them, and reflected it might be the last time I should behold them together on earth,—the last time I should be permitted to administer advice and consolation to their minds,—the last time I should have an opportunity to pour out my gratitude before them for the numerous manifestations of their confidence in my integrity, and appreciation of my humble service in their cause.

Searching as always for assurance of his own fame and vindication, and possessing a full measure of evangelical paternalism, Garrison could never truly grasp his black co-workers' motivation and feelings. Occasionally African American co-workers (usually male) would even tell him forthrightly that they resented his patronizing manner. But instead of deferring as he would to outspoken white women, he would contest their judgments with counterattacking accusations and expressions of wounded feelings. In Garrison's own world of abolitionism, Caucasian women, not African Americans of either gender, enjoyed the higher and more secure position.

In planning his trip to England Garrison thought carefully of his responsibilities, for his motives in making the journey were understandably ambitious. The British abolitionists were a source of enormous inspiration to their American counterparts in the early 1830s. Wealthy, socially dominant, and politically powerful, they seemed destined for imminent success as Parliament began debating bills of emancipation for all West Indian slaves. Speeches by prominent leaders such as William Wilberforce, Thomas Buxton, Henry Peter Brougham, and Thomas Clarkson furnished the nascent American crusaders with vital information and powerful formulations of emancipationist ideology. Most of all, the British example gave immediatists like Garrison a vivid sense that they had become involved in a relentless global crusade for humanity's liberation that stretched from India to the Caribbean, far overbalancing local reversals such as those in New Haven and Canterbury. Yet the British knew little about the budding American movement, what it stood for, or who its leaders were. What was even worse, an agent of the American Colonization Society, Elliot Cresson, was just then touring England and claiming to represent the best of antislavery opinion within the United States. For all these reasons, American immediatists eagerly sought to win the support of England's abolitionist luminaries. Garrison, of course, was no less anxious to secure their recognition as America's leading abolitionist, which could best be done by exposing the dangerous misrepresentation of Elliot Cresson.

As he prepared to sail, Garrison allowed his mind to fill with apocalyptic images that led him to visualize the magnitude of his future role, as he foresaw it, in a worldwide drama of emancipation. He wrote of experiencing a vision in which he stood nearly omniscient at a great height, overlooking all of Africa, the Atlantic Ocean, and the shores of North America. Below he could see thousands of native villages in flames and hear the "agonized groans" of the dying. Further out, he saw slave ships sailing to America, their wakes strewn with drowning and dead captives and their holds emitting "the cries of suffocating victims." And finally Garrison surveyed the United States, where he saw himself surrounded by an endless throng of supplicating slaves, "debased, weary, famished, bleeding and bound," begging him personally for their liberation. His ears then filled with the sound of an overpowering voice. *"Plead For The Oppressed,"* God thundered, to which replied Garrison, *"I must obey the voice from Heaven."*

It would be easy enough to dismiss this fantasy as simply one more flight of Garrison's unbridled ego (which of course it was) and miss its true importance. Traveling to England meant facing the problem of slavery from a global perspective, an entirely new horizon which expanded his quest for personal vindication as never before. Garrison's response, as his statement shows, was to redirect that global perspective back into his image of his own destiny, stimulating a dream of exerting the kind of unlimited power and purpose best known to charismatic religious leaders and apocalyptic political figures. Though Garrison had long struggled to reconcile personal sanctification with public success, his mission to England now led him to see himself as the leader of a worldwide millenium. Eagerly impatient to join the titans of British abolitionism, he sailed for Liverpool on May 1, 1833.

Soon after arriving, Garrison traveled to London and received a foretaste of the success that awaited him. His guide James Cropper had arranged introduction to a series of antislavery luminaries, beginning with Thomas Powell Buxton. When Garrison was presented, Buxton seemed puzzled, and then remarked: "Why my dear sir, I thought you were a black man! I have consequently invited this company of ladies and gentlemen to be present to welcome Mr. Garrison, the black advocate of emancipation from the United States of America." In light of Garrison's new found sense of his destiny, it is hardly surprising that he replied that Buxton's was the greatest compliment that

had ever been paid to him. Soon thereafter, he spent an afternoon each with Clarkson and the aging Wilberforce and was
thrilled to discover, ten days later, that Wilberforce and ten
other English worthies had published a statement condemning
the American Colonization Society and supporting immediatism instead.

Here was Garrison's perfect opening for launching a campaign to unmask Elliot Cresson and his Society to the rest of the
abolitionist world. Suddenly gone were any concerns about fulfilling the objectives he had announced when asking for money
from his African American supporters. The manual labor
school, he rationalized, could be funded exclusively by Americans since England seemed too afflicted by poverty to be able to
spare the cash. Then too, the actual prospect of begging before
members of the British peerage seemed to make Garrison
squirm with discomfort, a revealingly different reaction in contrast to his eagerness to solicit donations from humble church
groups in "Nigger Hill." By putting plans for the school aside in
order to expose Cresson's colonizationist deceptions to powerful
British allies, he would be aiding the entire cause, slaves as well
as free African Americans. Denunciation, not begging, would
more appropriately fulfill the prophetic duty to which he now
felt so strongly called.

Garrison challenged Cresson to an open debate, but Cresson
successfully avoided him. Throughout his own tour Cresson had
already been hounded repeatedly by another nettlesome immediatist, Charles Stuart, a close British friend of Theodore
Weld's, and he now had no stomach for facing Garrison. Failing
this, Garrison, Stuart, and Cropper, plus another zealous evangelical, George Thompson, with whom Garrison instantly became fast friends, attended a colonization rally and asked hostile
questions. They also organized a counter-meeting with Garrison as the featured speaker which took place on July 13 in Exeter
Hall. Garrison spoke for a full two hours to the best of the British abolitionists. The entire affair was all for which he had

dared to hope. Garrison opened his speech by attacking Cresson, outlining the charges presented in *Thoughts on Colonization*, and painting for his British listeners as terrible a picture of American slavery as his words could convey. Characterizing himself as sent "on an errand of mercy to plead for perishing millions," Garrison declared that the United States was "insulting the majesty of Heaven" by "professing to be the land of the free and the asylum of the oppressed" while disenfranchising a half-million free blacks, starving and plundering two million bondsmen, kidnapping untold numbers of newborn slaves, and "ruthlessly invading the holiest relations of life and cruelly separating the dearest ties of nature." What is more, by announcing that his "soul sicken[ed] in turning over this mass of corruption" and by criticizing the federal Constitution for protecting slavery, Garrison seemed to all but his most uncritical listeners to be calling not only for the overthrow of bondage, but also of the government of the United States. Before long, detractors would quote his words back to him, charging him as being a subversive turncoat in a British conspiracy to destroy America's social order by promoting slave insurrection and racial amalgamation.

For now, however, most English opinion hailed him as an antislavery hero. He had vanquished British support of colonization, cemented many new friendships, and made his name a byword among British reformers. As he boarded ship for the return to New York, his passage paid by a loan from yet another African American, Garrison was wholly unperturbed by any discomfort as to whose interests he had really served on this trip—his own or those of his many black benefactors. Because he meshed so completely his sense of prophetic destiny and drive to secure the public's notice with the millennium of black emancipation, such worries never occurred to him. Personal salvation and the freedom of the slaves were now more than ever nearly synonymous in his mind, and what seemed to matter most to achieve these ends was his newly acquired international renown.

Relying on this as well as his own private visions, he would now bring the British example to America and link New England to the worldwide crusade for the liberation of all humanity.

While Garrison had been traveling, abolitionists back home had been organizing, and by the fall of 1833 Arthur Tappan had emerged as the primary facilitator in publicizing and recruiting on behalf of the cause. He funded the production and mailing of antislavery publications that were sent to hundreds of ministers across the North. Using his wide networks of association he brought together and secured support from important evangelicals like William Jay, Joshua Leavitt, Amos Phelps, and William Goodell. By mail, he encouraged the Ohio abolitionist leaders—Weld, Beriah Green, and Elizur Wright, Jr.—to merge their efforts with his in developing a new antislavery society of unprecedented size. Meetings then followed with black activists such as Peter Williams, Samuel Cornish, and Theodore Wright. By the time Garrison debarked in New York City, news had reached America that the British had voted the emancipation of all West Indian slaves, and abolitionists agreed that the time was right to organize their own more broadly based antislavery society in the United States.

While Arthur Tappan organized, so did the abolitionists' opponents. West Indian emancipation had made a deep impression on Americans since Great Britain was universally recognized in the West as the world's most powerful nation and empire, and while abolitionists sought to emulate the British example, many others feared it greatly. With abolitionists now so active in America, their meddling British sponsors seemed capable of reaching into the very bowels of the nation to circulate the poisons of racial rebellion and sectional animosity. The specific British agents in question, of course, were "fanatics" like Arthur Tappan or worse still William Lloyd Garrison, who clearly had sold his loyalty to America's enemies in England by calling his own nation a "mass of moral corruption." To make matters worse, Garrison's debarkation point of New York City was always filled with visiting southern whites transacting business, northern merchants trading with the South, and a local, growing white working class which feared the economic and social consequences of emancipation. Freed slaves, they believed, would surely flee north to compete for their jobs in an already glutted unskilled labor market. Even before Garrison arrived from England, then, there were many who were saying that the best way to stop the "phrensy of Garrison and Arthur Tappan" was to "cut off their heads." Colonizationists, seeking revenge, well appreciated the diverse feelings that provoked this grim suggestion. So did secular-minded Jacksonian politicians and their lower class supporters. While there was significant working class support for abolition during the 1830s, many day laborers and artisans nevertheless saw in the "blue-nosed" evangelicals led by the Tappans a conspiracy to legislate compulsory church attendance, to banish the common man's right to a drink, to jeopardize their jobs by emancipating the slaves, and to enforce Christian moralism as the supreme law of the land.

On October 2, abolitionists assembled in New York City's Chatham Street Chapel and conducted their business quickly, while an angry mob advanced on the meeting from Tammany Hall, headquarters of the Democratic party. Some reformers exited through the back door; others hid in upstairs rooms, trapped by rioters behind locked doors until rescued by the police. Garrison claimed to have watched the melee from the street by posing as a spectator. But despite the mob's best effort the abolitionists managed to form their New York Anti-Slavery Society, cementing strong ideological and religious bonds only strengthened further by the common experience of martyrdom. The religious community of abolitionists was again expanding to incorporate an ever-wider range of temperaments and talents.

Theirs was, indeed, an impressive group. Both the Tappans, but especially Lewis, possessed a genius for organization and a shrewdness in assessing people that Garrison woefully lacked. Both brothers also had money and prestige that connected them directly to respectable evangelicals whom Garrison alone could have never reached, men of taste and distinction such as William Jay, son of the first Chief Justice of the Supreme Court of the United States, and Gerrit Smith, an upstate New York millionaire with vast real estate holdings who was soon to join the movement. Others of the Tappans' co-workers, Elizur Wright, Jr. and Joshua Leavitt, had skills for politics and management that were beyond Garrison's reach, and Theodore Weld surpassed everyone as abolitionism's peerless grass roots organizer. Yet Garrison supplied something of greatest importance too—a stringent standard of purity and acerbic style of denunciation that both challenged the timid and goaded the apathetic to commit themselves to the moral revolution. His statements outlining abolitionism's dramatic part in God's millennial designs endowed the crusade with rich and essential levels of spiritual expectation. The religion of abolitionism required a denunciatory and prophetic seer who stood independent of organizational management, and Garrison filled that role as no other could. Sensing their complimentary talents, Garrison and Lewis Tappan now pressed ahead with the British example by deciding to form a nationwide antislavery society at once.

Since the Quaker reformers who were Garrison's close friends needed to be drawn into the cause, the national convention took place in Philadelphia on December 4, 1833. The assembly yielded a revealing sample of the groups that were to lead the struggle for abolition over the next three decades. The Tappans, of course, spoke for the New York evangelicals and their offshoots in Ohio and upstate New York, including Jay, Weld, Leavitt, Amos A. Phelps, and Henry Brewster Stanton. Garrison headed a heterogenous delegation of New England Congregationalists like Ellis G. Loring, Unitarians like Samuel J. May and Samuel Sewall, and Quakers like Arnold Buffum, Joshua Coffin, and John Greenleaf Whitter. Quakers, in fact, accounted for twenty-one of the sixty-two delegates in attendance. Four women, all Quakers led by Lucretia Mott, attended (but not as delegates) while three black men, James McCrummel, Robert Purvis, and James Barbadoes, took full part in the official proceedings. Whatever their official roles, the presence of both groups testified to the significant contributions each was already making to the abolitionists' cause. Racially mixed and including both genders, the composition of the new American Anti-Slavery Society met Garrison's expectations perfectly. Yet their holy enterprise was clearly controlled by talented and aggressive white men, much like Garrison, who blended deep religious and humanitarian zeal with driving professional aspirations as editors, clerics, and businessmen.

Though Beriah Green presided over the meeting, Garrison dominated it, despite the fears of some of his new associates. Lewis Tappan and others, nervous that the controversial Bostonian might repel "many professed friends of abolition," tried to limit his official role by keeping him off major committees. Arthur Tappan became president, Lewis Tappan the chair of the executive committee, and Elizur Wright the secretary. Garrison was given the less exalted post of secretary of foreign correspondence, but he was also named to a subcommittee charged with drawing up a *Declaration of Sentiments* for the Society, and after some preliminary discussion May and Whittier left Garrison alone to work up the draft. Garrison reported his statement to the full meeting the following day, just after a speech by Lewis Tappan where he heard himself praised as a soul inspired by vision, courage, and necessary caution in his unflinching obedience to God's sternest dictates to seek justice. Tappan, the expert manager, had a full appreciation of Garrison's most valuable qualities.

For all its studied militance, Garrison's *Declaration* did strike a careful note of prudence for it made no call for bloodshed, civil disruption, or the defiance of laws. Because of this stress on nonviolence, the *Declaration* expressed quite eloquently those national goals for racial justice which most Americans even today would likely deem reasonable and consistent (at least in theory) with goals of the civil rights movements of the 1950s and 1960s. Firmly rejecting "the use of carnal weapons" by slaves or abolitionists, the *Declaration* emphasized that "doing evil [so] that good may come" was forbidden by Christian principles. Nonvi-

olence must be upheld even though the grievances held by slaves
against their masters made those of the American rebels against
England seem "trifling" by comparison: "Our forefathers were
never slaves—never bought and sold like cattle." Especially for
Americans who enjoyed such unique civil and religious liberty,
toleration of slavery constituted a sin "unequalled to any other
on the face of the earth." Every slaveholder stood convicted by
Scriptures as a "MANSTEALER" who had dared to "usurp the
prerogatives of Jehovah" by holding dominion over God's human creations.

Unshakable opposition to colonization, to compensated
emancipation, and to all laws upholding slavery was required to
overthrow the "monstrosity of bondage," proclaimed Garrison's
Declaration. Slaves, not their masters, deserved compensation
since the fruits of their labors had been stolen from them and
since they had always held the right to immediate freedom and
equal legal protection in the first place. Finally, in what was already proving the most difficult part of the abolitionist creed to
act on, signers of the *Declaration* pledged to battle race prejudice
whenever they found it, working to "secure," as Garrison put it,
"all rights and privileges that belong to all Americans," for "the
paths of preferment should be open as widely to them as to persons of white complexion."

To accomplish these formidable tasks, the *Declaration* urged
abolitionists to employ the crusading tactics of evangelical revivalism, relying on appeals to conscience, or "moral suasion" as
they called it, to stimulate the wholesale conversion of the
American mind. Haughty slaveholders, hate-filled racists, and
apathetic citizens everywhere must be forced to feel the crimi-
nality of their guilt, must be led to repent, and must be inspired
to enroll *en masse* in the ongoing moral revolution. To spread the
message, abolitionists should circulate antislavery literature
which was aimed at ministers and editors whose potent influence on the public would magnify the power of moral suasion;
clergymen, in particular must be made to embrace immediatism to inspire them to thunder at slaveholders from southern

pulpits and lead their entire congregations into the legions of the crusade. The American Anti-Slavery Society must also send agents throughout the free states to found new chapters in every city, town, and village. Finally, the Society should publish a national newspaper which would carry news of the abolitionist movement to readers all over America and throughout the British Empire. By all these means of moral suasion, the nation must be made to repent and be saved by the holy gospel of immediate emancipation. As Garrison wrote in the *Declaration*, the American Anti-Slavery Society was in its purest sense "dedicated to the destruction of error by the potency of truth—the overthrow of prejudice by the power of love—the abolition of slavery by the spirit of repentance."

After some revision of Garrison's more extreme phrases, Samuel J. May read the *Declaration* in its entirety, his voice shaking with emotion. "Our hearts were in perfect union," he recalled. "There was but one thought with us all. We thought the word had just been uttered which would be mighty, through God, to the pulling down of the strongholds of slavery." Silence then reigned as the delegates filed one by one up to the platform to affix their signatures. Garrison's deep sense of the prophet's role to which he had been called had been, he felt, fully confirmed. Presidencies and other high offices could be left to day-to-day administrators like the Tappans. Independent as always, Garrison would instead continue in the *Liberator* to arm abolition with warrants from the Divine, defying all opponents and prophesying victory.

To most Americans, Garrison's *Declaration of Sentiments* was unmitigated fanaticism. Yet for all this visionary radicalism, his words also echoed and reinforced some of the dominant social and economic trends of his age by asserting that each person, regardless of race, must be "secure in his right to his body—to the protections of law—to the product of his own labor—to the common advantage of society." In this respect the *Declaration* magnified tenants of economic self-reliance to which many other citizens subscribed and which had begun transforming

America into a nationally integrated economy propelled by individualistic capitalism. It insisted with great emphasis that every individual possessed the inalienable right to advance by his own efforts and condemned an oppressive relationship that destroyed an individual's freedom to compete for the fulfillment of his own destiny. As a self-liberated devotee of Benjamin Franklin, so fiercely possessive of his own independence, Garrison shared this belief in economic individualism with Andrew Jackson, who battled banking monopolies, with Whigs who resisted Jackson's presidential "tyranny," with Antimasons who dismantled secret societies, with temperance advocates who exposed conspiring liquor interests, and with nativists who crusaded against the Roman Catholic church.

What distinguished Garrison and his colleagues from all these other groups was their extraordinary demand that over two million humans, representing an investment of many billions of dollars, be instantly transformed into productive and self-reliant citizens. Immediatism, in this respect, projected the opening of a totally new era of Christian prosperity, equality, and harmony throughout the nation, a competitive society unparalleled in its inclusiveness where biblical morality, unimpeded social mobility, and personal autonomy would benefit and uplift all Americans, whether white or black. The trumpet call of immediate emancipation would thus accelerate the emergence of the United States as a modern nation of competitive capitalists, led by men who equated their new idea of racial equality with an ever-expanding commitment to individual freedom. In this respect Garrison and his fellow abolitionists were exactly what they conceived of themselves to be—the prophets of a new age.

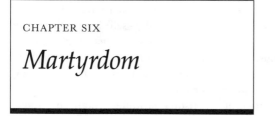

CHAPTER SIX

Martyrdom

Garrison, now twenty-nine, first met the woman he would marry just before leaving for England in 1834, when Helen Benson and her father George attended one of his fundraising lectures in Providence, Rhode Island. George Benson was a distinguished Quaker patriarch possessing antislavery credentials dating to the 1790s. At age eighty-two, he had just succeeded Arnold Buffum as President of the New England Anti-Slavery Society, and his two sons, George, Jr. and Henry, were also firm abolitionists and Quakers. Their twenty-three-year-old sister had been schooled to hate slavery since her earliest years. The family farm in Brooklyn, Connecticut, known as Friendship's Valley, had long been a gathering place for reformers, and Helen had ample opportunity to become acquainted with most of Garrison's colleagues. Within a week of their first meeting Garrison departed for England, but a year later he was courting her with a determined eye to marriage.

His demanding emotional makeup and damaging family relationships must have made the prospect of intimacy a difficult challenge for Garrison. His serious feelings for Helen began to grow, in fact, just as Prudence Crandall was giving him so full a reminder of the power of strong-minded women. Crandall's Canterbury school was located close to the Benson's farm, and Garrison, Crandall, and Helen Benson were briefly friends before the headstrong schoolmistress and the patronizing editor had their falling out. Angered and intimidated by Crandall's display of independence, Garrison may well have turned with relief to Helen Benson, who was shy, self-deprecating, and calmly practical. Above all, Helen's first instincts were supportive and generous, the antithesis of Fanny Garrison's self-seeking possessiveness. Always conscious of the memory of his mother, Garrison chose to marry her opposite.

The complexities of Garrison's attitudes toward marriage, however, went beyond an aversion to a domineering spouse. In his youth, of course, he had posed as an Old Bachelor, deriding marriage as the greatest trammel of all to the sense of independence he always craved. "Marriage," he had written, was "instituted to please the commonality—not to shackle the scholar, the philosopher, the statesman, the warrior....Families are so many cares which distract the mind, weaken the strength and tame the fire of genius." Although these warnings may reflect memories of his troubled parents, they also suggest a deeper ambivalence. Garrison, plainly, had strong physical desires for women, yet the demands of self-control, so thoroughly ingrained in him since his childhood, quarreled deeply with his sexual nature. Only when Garrison felt completely secure in the company of a close male friend could he even suggest the outlines of his erotic feelings. For example, he confessed in 1829 to brief infatuation with a certain Mary Cunningham and then wrote suggestively to his good friend Stephen S. Foster to share a fantasy he had about applying cosmetics to her face:

Hold your head steadily, dearest—so—very still—you shall look in the glass presently—a little more vermilion, a denser flame of health on this cheek—I like to see the blood, Mary, mounting up to the very temple, co-mingling with that lily whiteness—your eyebrows are hardly coal black—a little darker, in order to give a deeper brilliance to your starry eyes, or rather to their light—shut your mouth, and draw back that little saucy tongue, you pretty witch, for I'm going to put a ruby blush upon your twin (not thin) lips, after I've kissed them—there—softly—softly—smack goes the brush...Cetera desunt.

In his public writings during the same period Garrison presented himself in a much more ambiguous and self-controlled
fashion. In one instance, An Old Bachelor wrote poetically of
the torture of unrequited love and the solace of death by suicide.
At other times, in both the *Free Press* and the *National Philanthropist*
he meshed the roles of the heartbroken lover and the disillusioned bachelor, lamenting the fickleness and vanity of women.
Through the posture of a pure sentimentalist made wise by the
pain of romantic tragedy he could reveal himself to be deeply
drawn to women, yet far too cautious and wronged to seek their
intimacy. This wary stance, of course, also protected him
against abiding fears of rejection and humiliation that colored
so strongly his emotional makeup.

Given this background, Garrison was terribly nervous when
first approaching even the kind and unassertive Helen Benson.
After returning from England, he visited the Benson family in
March of 1834, and upon meeting Helen again he recalled,
"My tongue was tied and my heart timorous and so I was
dumb." All this was natural enough, and his next step was
equally hesitant. Upon arriving home after the visit he sent her
a most ambiguous letter, offering his "whole heart" not to Helen, but to *all* the Benson family, while cryptically asking,
"Have you anything in the *shape of a heart* to give me, Helen?"
Fearful of his own instincts and the possible humiliation of rejection, he succeeded in confusing Helen rather than wooing her.
She replied simply that Garrison might find her unworthy of his
friendship, a response which left Garrison at a loss. In his first
attempt to hint at his love he seemed to hope that she would
make the first open demonstration; when that failed he went on,
undeterred, to appeal this time to her maternal solicitude and
generosity.

When next he wrote, he pictured himself as a frail and vulnerable soul. "I weep as easily as a babe, am as sensitive as a flower,
and as aerial as a bird," he assured her, recalling the "cloud of
melancholy" that had "fallen over [his] breast within the past
few days." Much as his mother had done to him so many years

before, he pleaded for Helen's pity. He recalled the lonely feelings that had overcome him during his tour of England, even as he was being welcomed and cheered by friends and admirers. "Among them all," he remembered himself lamenting, "was there not one who cherished toward me aught beyond friendship's affection?"

> And therefore I wept in sadness and solitude. Is it ever thus to be? Alas, all may be mated but me—I have no attraction to enkindle or secure love—there is none in this wide world whose heart I am authorized to claim—none in whose bosom I can pour the wealth of my affection.

The hint was all too blatant, and Helen, now fulfilling the accommodating role that she would continue to play throughout Garrison's life, took it at once. Answering his lamentation that he had "no attractions to kindle or secure love," she sweetly confessed "*I never saw one that possessed more*—for they have completely entwined themselves around my heart, and the connecting link, I trust, death can only dissolve."

He had enticed Helen to make the first open avowals of love, yet even this reversal of roles did not assure Garrison that his purity and independence had been upheld. While accepting joyously Helen's heartfelt declaration, he also began assuming the role of spiritual mentor almost immediately by reminding her that "there is one who we love and admire more than we do each other—*and only one*." Love of God must come before all human love, he warned her, adding (with complete obliviousness of the monumental irony of his words) that she must always beware the temptations of self-infatuation: "We should meekly bend like the reed to the breath of eulogy, but be lofty and unyielding as the OAK when the tempest of unrighteous persecution is raging around us. How contemptible, how foolish, how disgusting is personal egotism!" He also strove to assure himself of his own purity by emphasizing to Helen the sanctity of his "passionate attachment" to her: "I remember nothing with which to upbraid myself; for I love you with a pure heart and would not for worlds behave unseemly in your sight." In marriage as well as courtship there would be no explosion of the volatile feelings that had destroyed his family years before. True passion, the love that received God's blessing, was reserved only for those who submitted with gladness to the dictation of His higher laws.

Marriage, in short, would become for Garrison yet another opportunity of self-emancipation, intimately connecting his most personal relationship to the cause of abolition. He drew the connection explicitly for Helen, asserting that the spiritual inspiration of their wedded love would only lead him to battle all the more fiercely for slavery's overthrow: "I ought to plead more earnestly and eloquently now than ever, because I can realize how dreadful a thing it is for lover to be torn away from lover, the husband from the wife, parents from children." And on a more personal level still, Garrison looked to his marriage to reconcile as nothing else could his public role as a harsh and defiant prophet with his deepest feelings of sentiment and tenderness: "Dear Helen," he wrote, "am I not a strange compound? In battling with the whole nation I am as impetuous, as daring, as unconquerable as a lion; but in your presence I am as gentle and submissive as a dove." Other abolitionist couples too were to see in their marriages striking metaphors of personal submission and mutual liberation that enriched their dedication to the religion of immediatism. By linking married love so directly to the struggle for black emancipation, Garrison was hardly unique. Yet once again his emancipation and that of the slaves had become wholly intertwined, a powerful fusion of personal life with public mission that could only inspire him all the more to challenge a blaspheming nation. With the promise of God's blessings on his new house, Lloyd himself felt compelled all the more to shout defiance at the corruption that he sensed crowding in around it.

In Helen, Garrison also finally found liberation of a much different sort, for with her, as perhaps with no other, he could let down his defenses, relax, and give way to the playful side of his nature. The security of their commitment, based as it was on Helen's constant compliance, fortified his self-assurance as nothing else could. He began to fill his letters to her and to other close friends with questionable puns, bad jokes, snatches of inaccurately quoted poetry, and his own endlessly saccharine verses. All his life he was to delight in playing with words in this fashion, often displaying a zestful sense of humor that too often escaped the notice of contemporaries and historians as well. Writing, for example, of a *"black and white cat,"* offered to him as a gift which he refused, he observed that as "I am opposed to colonization, let the little sable animal remain until I visit Boston. I may possibly volunteer to sonnet upon it bye and bye—especially if a *cat*-astropy overtake it, so that I might say "Requis-*cat* in pace" in conveying its mortal remains to the *cat*-acombs." On another occasion he inflicted on Helen a seemingly endless, pun-filled ode to a Thanksgiving turkey. For Garrison, marriage to Helen would lead to the rich reconciliation of public with private identity for which he had hoped, freeing him to express spontaneous laughter at home and denunciation before the world. "I did not marry her," he later wrote of Helen, "expecting she would assume a prominent station in the antislavery cause, but for domestic quiet and happiness." Helen, for her part, would always respond to her domineering husband with patient agreement, for she truly loved him, as she confessed "a thousand times more than my tongue can ever utter." Little wonder that Garrison chose the name "Freedom's Cottage" to be the name of their new home.

On Thursday, September 4, 1834, Samuel J. May officiated at Helen and Lloyd's wedding, held in the morning at the Bensons' Friendship Valley. By ten o'clock the ceremony had ended, and Lloyd and Helen were seated in a comfortable carriage, ready to begin their two-day trip to their new home in Roxbury, just outside Boston. Accompanying them were Garrison's maternal aunt, Charlotte Lloyd, and Elizabeth Chace, Helen's best friend. Upon their arrival in Roxbury, they were joined by Abigail and Isaac Knapp, whom Garrison had invited to spend two weeks as they set up housekeeping in Freedom's Cottage. Garrison had never known a family that could reassure and sustain him, or one to which he could contribute freely as a confident personality. But now, thanks to Helen, he felt a growing sense of belonging which could encompass not only close friends like the Knapps, but the entire Benson clan as well. The genial host of Freedom's Cottage opened its doors from the very first to an endless stream of houseguests, and Helen, so far as is known, never protested. "Your humility charms me," Garrison once revealed to her, "and your good sense and wise judgment redound to your credit." It is little wonder that he loved her, since her primary focus was to support her husband in every way possible.

While Helen and Lloyd sought domestic tranquility, the world outside Freedom's Cottage could fairly be said to be exploding in violent upheaval. After the formation of the American Anti-Slavery Society in 1833, abolitionists found themselves facing an ever-increasing tempo of harassment, repression, and mob violence that quickened in intensity between 1834 and 1838. When Garrison had first published the *Liberator* in 1831 his denunciations had not incited Bostonians to violence, even in the aftermath of the Nat Turner insurrection. But by 1834, not just the vituperative Garrison but any abolitionist, no matter how soft-spoken, risked personal safety by speaking publicly on emancipation. The character of American political culture had changed dramatically as the decade progressed, and suddenly violence was an all-too-common and accepted feature of everyday life.

Though abolitionists were in part the cause of the wave of repression that swept over them, they were nevertheless hardly the only group victimized by a society that now seemed to welcome violent solutions to its deeper anxieties. Repeated acts of group violence against abolitionists, Masonic lodges, banks, Catholic convents, African American communities, and even yellow fever hospitals took place so frequently in the mid 1830s that some began to fear a total disintegration of the nation's social order. To many citizens the ethos of the period even supported these outbursts, emphasizing as they did for the first time the individual's power to participate in the ongoing shaping of public life. Mob action was seen by some as simply a logical extension of the political rally or the ballot box, another more direct way to protect society from such disruptive agents as Catholics, Masons, bankers, African Americans and abolitionists. Rioters regarded their actions as a patriotic defense of the existing order, never subversive, for they were simply acting with speed to protect popular rule and individual rights from insidious groups that mayors and politicians seemed powerless to restrain.

But violence against abolitionists also arose from specific anxieties stimulated by their activities, and by late 1833, those who would riot against them were developing many strong reasons of their own for fear and opposition. By the close of that year, abolitionism could easily be regarded as a disruptive and growing conspiracy of British and American firebrands, for the movement had expanded from four local societies in two states to forty-seven in ten states stretching from Indiana to Maine, and was run by dozens of talented managers, authors, and editors. Supported, many believed, by the Tappans' fabled wealth and Garrison's malevolent British compatriots, the abolitionists seemed able to make their unwelcome presence felt in every corner of the nation. And in 1834, they indeed began a "great postal campaign" as they called it, flooding the republic, north and south, with literally hundreds of thousands of tracts, periodicals, and sermons. With Garrison's constant support through the *Liberator*, itinerant abolitionist agents fanned out throughout the North, appearing without invitation in cities and towns everywhere to question ministers, challenge colonizationists, found antislavery societies, and establish abolitionist newspapers. Without seeking the approval of local authorities, abolitionists began circulating, hand to hand, petitions to Congress demanding the abolition of the internal slave trade and of slavery in the District of Columbia.

Most disturbing of all, according to their opponents, abolitionists had begun collaborating with free blacks, seeming thereby to substantiate the most worrisome fears of racial amalgamation and the destruction of the white social order. White skin, more than anything else, served to mute the ever-widening economic gulf between rich and poor that was developing in Jacksonian America, giving stable identity to whites otherwise caught in the shifting circumstances of their socially fluid age. From the wealthiest colonizationist to the poorest day laborer, a formidable body of northern citizens had reasons in abundance to view bitterly Garrison, Tappan, and their ilk as meddlesome and dangerous outsiders who must be put down. Joining in these sentiments, of course, were those other whites throughout the South who responded to the abolitionists' campaign with vehement protests and acts of violence of their own.

The mobs struck first in New York City in July 1834, when rioters fiercely and effectively suppressed an abolitionist meeting by vandalizing parts of the black community and burning Lewis Tappan's house to the ground. Soon thereafter George Thompson, fresh from Great Britain, appeared at Garrison's invitation to begin a year-long speaking tour. Thompson presented a perfect target for mob action, an indisputable British "agent" of abolitionism who seemed to reek with foreign arrogance, a sarcastic and vehement speaker carrying Garrison's most fulsome endorsements in the *Liberator*. As he moved from town to town in New England, violence greeted him—brickbats in Concord, New Hampshire; garbage, raw eggs, and rocks in Lowell, Massachusetts. Fleeing New England, Thompson headed with hope to Ohio and found even less hospitable audiences. More than once he was threatened with lynching and was seriously injured when hit in the face with a stone. Now more a fugitive than a lecturer, Thompson finally returned to Boston in October 1835 and made his escape to England in secret, fearing he might be kidnapped before he left. Garrison grew genuinely frightened and deeply dismayed by these outbursts, particularly since he felt responsible for the plight of Thompson, his personal guest. As the repression continued, he began urging his fellow abolitionists to stop making public speeches, for "there is too much fever, and too little rationality to permit any of us to address the patient without having him attempt to knock us down." But his advice had little practical impact, for in the South as well as the North the level of violence continued to rise.

Angry mobs in South Carolina and Washington, D.C. tore open mailbags, searching for abolitionist literature. Throughout the slave states planters united in their opposition by mustering militia, convening "indignation meetings," demanding Garrison's extradition, and holding mock lynchings. Isolated southern immediatists such as James G. Birney were forced to flee to the North, while northern abolitionists caught traveling in the South were flogged and jailed. And even when Birney arrived in Cincinnati and attempted to start an abolitionist newspaper there, rioters hurled his press into the Ohio River. A mob in Utica, New York, broke up an antislavery meeting by attacking several delegates, and Weld's band of abolitionist organizers were met by rioters and marauders as they moved eastward from Ohio. Most frightening of all, perhaps, was the federal government's reaction towards the abolitionists' activities and the nation's resultant sharp turn toward lawlessness. In his annual message to Congress, President Andrew Jackson, a slaveholding Tennesseean, voiced approval of this southern white resistance and urged Congress to ban all abolitionist literature from the mails. Though Congress rejected Jackson's suggestions, the House of Representatives did pass a highly controversial gag rule which made it impossible to report or debate antislavery petitions on the floor of Congress.

Meanwhile, in Boston, the talented author and newly recruited Garrisonian Lydia Maria Child imagined that the nation was passing through "scenes like those of the French Revolution," when mobs terrified honest citizens and people were afraid to trust even their closest neighbors. Certainly Boston's African Americans had reason aplenty for distrusting their fellow citizens, for during the summer of 1835 bands of thugs repeatedly attacked their churches and homes. Editors filled their pages with condemnations of Thompson and Garrison, and on

August 31 citizens filled Faneuil Hall to overflowing to listen to Harrison Gray Otis condemn the abolitionists. Seeing the clear threat when someone erected a stout gallows in front of his home, Garrison attacked his old hero in the *Liberator* but chose not to show himself at Otis's meeting. Rumors circulated, as he wrote Henry Benson, that "assassins legalized by States Rights Governments" had been sent undercover to Boston "to destroy me."

In the midst of this uproar, the Boston Female Anti-Slavery Society decided to hold its annual meeting as scheduled on October 14. Rumors had it that Thompson would be the principal speaker, though Thompson, in fact, was out of the city. On the day of the meeting, hundreds of inflammatory handbills began circulating the demand that "the infamous foreign scoundrel Thompson...be brought to the tar kettle before dark," and Mayor Theodore Lyman prepared for trouble. When Garrison arrived at the Anti-Slavery Hall around two o'clock, a large crowd of hecklers had gathered outside, and an equal number within had cornered the women in rooms on the third floor. He pushed his way through the crowd and up the stairs, meeting threats but no attacks, and sat himself with the racially mixed membership of the Society, insisting at first that the intruders leave. When he then realized the extent of his own danger, Garrison hurriedly retired to an office and locked the door behind him.

Mayor Lyman arrived soon after with a body of policemen and told everyone to disperse, especially since George Thompson would not be appearing. Although the regal and wealthy Maria Weston Chapman wanted to stand firm—"If this is the last bulwark of freedom we may as well die here," she declared—the women did adjourn, leaving Garrison alone with the mob. Thinking quickly, he crawled out a back window and jumped into the street, but the crowd outside glimpsed him and the chase began. After dodging into a carpenter's shop, he was quickly cornered in a second-floor room. One of his captors started to wrestle him towards the window, intending to hurl

him to the street, but others with better judgment prevailed and
began coiling a thick rope around his body, probably intending
to drag him to the "tar kettle" once meant for Thompson. At
this juncture, Garrison was able to make his escape outside into
the welcoming arms of several daring sympathizers. With the
assistance of Lyman's constables, they wrestled him through the
frenzied crowd to safety, much of his clothing being torn in the
process. From there he was quickly shipped by coach for his own
protection to the Leverett Street jail, where he cheerfully spent
the evening and entertained guests. As in Baltimore, he explained his physical incarceration as a testimony to his spiritual
freedom, and inscribed on the wall the statement that he, William Lloyd Garrison, had been confined in this jail for "preaching the abominable and dangerous doctrine that all men had
been created equal." Even his opponents agreed that he had
conducted himself with brave dignity throughout his ordeal,
true at all times to his pacifist principles.

In many respects, in fact, the Boston mob of 1835 and the
larger wave of repression it exemplified appeared as a godsend
to the abolitionists. For Garrison personally the mobs railing
against him and the threats from the South furnished abundant
opportunities for him to exhibit once again his unconquerable
independence by hurling defiance at his detractors. He also discovered that unpopularity and denunciations were finally beginning to sell newspapers, increasing his income as well as his
reputation. Following the riots, subscriptions to the still-
struggling *Liberator* picked up markedly, and the paper's circulation, though still modest, now promised to make it self-
sustaining. More important still, some of these new readers
were also significant new recruits, propelled into the cause by
their hostile reaction to the violence. The brilliant Boston patrician, Wendell Phillips, soon to become Garrison's closest friend
and one of abolitionism's most gifted thinkers and orators,
found the Boston riot deeply disturbing and began suspecting
that slavery, not the abolitionists, was plunging the nation into
disorder and despotism. Two years later, when a mob in Alton,

Illinois, murdered abolitionist editor Elijah Lovejoy, Phillips would make his dramatic public entry into the cause. Wealthy Gerrit Smith, moved by similar concerns, now joined the American Anti-Slavery Society as well. So did several others who were soon to become close friends of Garrison's, three Boston "Brahmins"—Edmund Quincy, Dr. Henry Bowditch, and George B. Emerson—and an obscure Connecticut hatmaker, Henry Clarke Wright.

Such conversions, important as they were, diminished in significance when compared to the spread of strong antislavery feelings throughout many parts of the North. Southern repression, northern mob violence, and above all the shocking murder of Elijah Lovejoy now began to make many northern whites who cared little for black emancipation worry deeply about the safety of their own civil liberties. The disrupted meetings, the rifled mail bags, the rioting, the gag rule, and the widespread high level of repression seemed increasingly to indicate that powerful slaveholders and their supporters harbored total contempt for everyone else's freedom but their own and were striving to protect their corrupt interests by crushing liberty not only in the South but now in the North as well. The abolitionists were now beginning to capture the sympathies of many northerners simply because the violence against them was giving new credence to their cause. "How the heathen rage," wrote an exultant Samuel J. May to Garrison during the height of the violence. "Our opponents are doing everything to help us." Never before, May thought, had any subject "been so much talked about as slavery is everywhere," and the abolitionists were quick to take advantage of the rising new concern in the North for civil rights. "The liberties of those yet free are in imminent peril," warned James G. Birney from Ohio. "It is not only for the emancipation of the slaves that we contend."

Aware from the first of this significant new trend, Garrison was nevertheless very suspicious of those whites who were now coming late to the abolitionists' cause while caring most of all for their own civil liberties. "The time has gone by," he observed to Lewis Tappan, "for men to manifest extraordinary courage or disinterestedness in the cause of the slave. We shall constantly see 'great men' coming in at the death of the monster slavery now that we have given him a mortal wound." In Garrison's view, six years of agitation had hardly set off the moral revolution that he had so anticipated. Instead, a much more ambiguous, equivocal, and slow-moving sort of progress could be seen going forward in the North, a new form of antislavery based on a deep suspicion of slaveholder's values and their impact on the nation's republican freedom, yet equally leery of immediate emancipation. But whatever an abolitionist's estimate of the meaning of these trends, it was incontestable that they had succeeded in making the practice of slaveowning an issue that Americans could no longer ignore.

Garrison, however, was not one to believe that even the slowest of progress was actually being made. Though he welcomed the converts and the notoriety, the violence itself angered, threatened, and repelled him very deeply. From childhood he had detested all evidence of uncontrolled passion, rejecting it as the source of chaos and degradation that had cursed his family and now condemned the nation through the abomination of chattel slavery. Little wonder, when faced with direct physical threats from mobs or hooligans, that he would never respond in kind, resorting to editorial combat instead. As when he had faced the Boston mob, he always remained the picture of calm in such trying situations, his disdain of violence permitting him to distance himself completely from the unchecked turbulence he so hated. In private, too, he always shrugged off all threats of physical harassment. "My mind is at peace," he once commented. "I know what it is to rejoice in tribulation. Give me brickbats in the cause of God," he proclaimed, "to wedges of gold in the cause of sin." Though these were the words of a self-vindicating martyr, they also reflected Garrison's growing desire to set himself apart still further from a world which disturbed him deeply, one that was revealing itself as far more violently corrupted than even he had first imagined.

The same unsettling discoveries and disappointments also drove Garrison to set increasingly rigid boundaries around abolitionism as a sanctified and separate religious fellowship. In earlier times, he had expected his moral revolution to sweep all before it, even predicting complete emancipation within the course of the decade. But instead, moral suasion had served only to provoke a repression that had left slavery still entrenched while undermining the nation's moral foundations. "When we first unfurled the banner of the *Liberator*," Garrison confessed in late 1835, "we did not anticipate that to protect Southern slavery the free states would voluntarily trample underfoot all law, order and government, or brand the advocates of universal liberty as incendiaries." Deeply repelled by this frightening turn of events, he began clinging all the more firmly to the fellowship of the cause itself, regarding the American Anti-Slavery Society as a purified body of believers who gave one another both sanctuary and inspiration when facing a turbulent nation that had snapped all ties to Christian morality.

As reports of mob violence continued to reach him, Garrison's mind began filling with analogies that linked the abolitionists' travails with those of the church's first martyrs. "As in the days of the Early Christians," he wrote, proscription and terrorism were uniting the immediatists "in a common bond, as one man...in one unbroken phalanx." Their movement alone, he declared in 1835, enrolled "the genuine disciples of Christ," for it was proving itself a far more righteous fellowship of Christians than any conventional denomination or church. "We are constantly purified in the furnace of affliction," he claimed, using a typical Old Testament analogy, "and the dross is taken away. The risks that we run, the odium we receive, the persecution we suffer" bore most authentic witness of all, he believed, to the sanctity of the abolitionists' godly fellowship and assured the vindication of their holy cause. To continue the struggle against a fallen world, "we must crucify all our sectarian prejudices," Garrison wrote, "and combat valiantly for God and Truth, counting not our character, or property or our lives dear to us, for with Christ's strengthening we can do all things, even to the extermination of American slavery and prejudices."

New England's most prominent spokesmen for Protestantism, Lyman Beecher and William Ellery Channing, seemed to give Garrison every reason for making these provocative claims. In September 1835, his former spiritual mentor Beecher tried to stifle the American Anti-Slavery Society by creating an organization of his own, the American Union for the Relief and Improvement of the Colored Race, which pledged itself in the vaguest of phrases to gradual emancipation. Though Garrison condemned it and the effort soon collapsed, Beecher's attempt made it very clear that evangelical denominations were emphatically rejecting immediate emancipation. Soon thereafter, Unitarian William Ellery Channing joined the ranks of those deemed apostates by Garrison by publishing his *Thoughts on Slavery*. While Channing did adopt some abolitionist thinking he, like Beecher, also rejected immediate emancipation and racial equality as fool's errands and terrible threats to society. Garrison scorned Channing's position as "*sheer moral* plagiarism . . . a farrago of impertinence, contradiction and defamation," and was especially shocked to discover that some of his abolitionist brethren, particularly Samuel J. May and Ellis Gray Loring, considered the work "worthy of extensive circulation and extreme panegyric." Fearing that the religion of abolitionism was now being infiltrated by heresy, he publicly attacked Channing's *Thoughts* with a venom uncommon even for him.

Finally, it was Beecher once again who gave Garrison a last shred of confirmation as to the wholly corrupted nature of the nation's religious leadership. In July 1836 Beecher delivered a widely discussed sermon defending the sanctity of the Sabbath, the authority of the Bible, and the leadership of the ordained clergy as the surest bulwark against the corruptions of party politics, materialism, irreligion, and fanaticism that he feared were besetting the nation. A zealous ordained clergy, Beecher emphasized, must strive tirelessly to enforce the moral law against godless disorganizers of every sort whether immoral politicos or frenzied abolitionists, both of whom had unleashed dangerous trends that were unraveling the national fabric. To Garrison, Beecher's sermon illustrated perfectly the spiritual blindness that now afflicted all organized religion, and in five closely printed columns in the *Liberator* he castigated it mercilessly while setting forth some new and very iconoclastic doctrines that he had now begun to formulate.

The Sabbath, Garrison argued, possessed no shred of scriptural authority, and Beecher's attempt to uphold it was simply an impious human invention that masked the true Christian's obligation to be "constantly in the service of God. . . . Let men consecrate to the service of Jehovah not *one* day in seven, but in *all* their thoughts, actions and powers," Garrison contended. By upholding the meaningless technicalities of religious formalism, Beecher actually was giving "his protective influence to a system of slavery and heathenism which, at a single blow, annihilates the whole decalogue and. . .excludes from the benefits of the Sabbath two million and a half countrymen!" Only if false-hearted Christians would "put on Christ" daily as an example of sanctified living "may they be as free as the Master" of sin, for "He is Lord even on the Sabbath day."

Urgent and disturbing notes of anticlericalism and religious perfectionism had now begun to surface in Garrison's religious thinking, accurate barometers of his rapidly deepening alienation from the nation's predominant Protestant institutions and doctrines. In editorial after editorial he castigated the Protestant clergy as "disgraces to humanity. . .heathenish, filled with apologies for sin and sinners of the worst sort. . .Bulwarks of Slavery . . .[and] accessories to the MANSTEALERS in the bloodiest of their crimes." In private too, he began to lament over the "partial, *dwarfed* and corrupted" state of organized religion, "now that the churches and Presbyteries and Synods are unanimously voting that slavery is divinely sanctioned and may properly be perpetuated." "Oh the rottenness of Christendom!" he exclaimed to Samuel J. May in mid-1836. "I am forced to believe that, as respects the greater proportion of professing Christians in this land, Christ has died in vain." Conscious of his growing estrangement from established institutions, Garrison used the occasion of his thirtieth birthday to reassess his mission as well as the direction of his career. His hopes now blasted for the speedy emancipation that would vindicate his purity and vision, Garrison's thinking was taking some radical directions that help to encompass his growing anticlericalism. "Much as my mind is absorbed in the antislavery cause," he revealed to his sister-in-law Anna Benson, he now believed that there were also "other great subjects upon which much light must be thrown, and which are of utmost importance to the temporal and eternal welfare of man."

Garrison had always conceived of himself as a "universal reformer," active in the causes of temperance, the Sabbath, women's rights, and peace as well as abolition. But now, he was deciding that those issues together with slavery must all be addressed at once by sanctified Christian reformers who had embraced the doctrine of nonresistance. Those who would be true servants of the religion of abolition must now, before all else, separate themselves entirely from the repressive influences of church and state, those powers which had now been proven to spawn warfare, encourage mobs, suppress African Americans, and dominate women. "I am more and more convinced," he explained to Benson, "that it is the duty of the followers of Christ to suffer to be defrauded, calumniated, and barbarously treated without resorting to their own physical energies, or the force of law for restitution and punishment." A violence-ridden political system and a clerical establishment that wallowed in blasphemy could only be vanquished by those who embodied their complete moral opposite by rejecting all allegiances to such corrupting institutions. As he pressed forward in his lifelong quests for sanctification and vindication, Garrison saw the perfect example of Jesus Christ as now suggesting some far more radical remedies for a nation so terribly mired in sin. By rejecting organized religion in this fashion, the independence bred of spiritual self-emancipation was once again his, freeing him from the manifest failure of moral suasion alone to overcome violence and repression. "Blessed be to God that I am not entangled in this yoke of bondage," he wrote exaltedly to May, "and that I am not allied with them in spirit or form."

The doctrines of nonresistance and religious perfectionism thus served to answer all his perplexing questions and speak to his deepest feelings of alienation. What could the violence signify but the hollowness of all conventional religion and the barrenness of American political culture? How could abolitionists hope to save themselves from these polluting influences and secure their overthrow while still faithfully obeying God's will as apostles of emancipation? The answer, to Garrison, was finally becoming reduced to the simple biblical injunction, "Be ye perfect, even as your heavenly Father is perfect." Members of the church of immediate emancipation would have to repudiate as sinful all forms of human coercion, "put on the garment of Christ," and hurl defiance at every godless claim of church and state.

By the spring of 1837, Garrison's perfectionist thinking had advanced quite far when he met John Humphrey Noyes, a spiritual seeker who met his every qualification. A visionary who far exceeded even Garrison in audacity, Noyes had already begun to propound his belief that a sanctified social system could be assembled in which spiritually perfected human beings submitted themselves entirely to God's flawless will. In Noyes's view, heaven and earth could become one, and no need would exist for such coercive institutions as civil government, private property, organized religion, or legally enforced marriage. As he explained to Garrison, sinful human governments could make absolutely no claims for obedience on those who had truly "put on the mantle of Christ," and neither could corrupted churches. Every act of political repression and clerical denunciation of which Garrison now complained so bitterly, Noyes assured him, arose as the inevitable consequence of godlessly coercive institutions. When Noyes pictured the government of the United States he saw, as he told Garrison, "a bloated, swaggering libertine, trampling on the Bible—on its Constitution, on its treaties with Indians—the petitions of its citizens; with one hand whipping a negro, tied to a liberty pole, with the other dashing an emaciated Indian to the ground." The nation's government must be anathema to the perfect Christian and must be overthrown before all humanity, slaves included, could truly become emancipated. As Noyes explained it, the godless authority of southern masters over their black slaves could be found repeated and magnified throughout all unsanctified human relationships and social institutions. Submission to the worldly discipline of governments, political parties, law codes, ministers, legally enforced marriages, or even one's own private passion was a defiance of God's will no less blatant than owning one of His human creations. It behooved Garrison at once, Noyes urged him, to declare his freedom from the government of the United States in terms that Christ himself had sanctified—the nonresistant language of renunciation and prophetic defiance. By coming out of sinful relationships, abolitionists themselves would cease to be accessories to evil and thus purified, could once again be fit and empowered to begin anew the moral revolution. "Your station is a high one that gives you power over the nation," Noyes exhorted Garrison. "If you love your posts of honor—the forefront of the righteous battle—set your face toward *perfect* holiness." For Garrison, slave emancipation and personal liberation had always been undistinguishable. But through perfectionism, Noyes had fully demonstrated just how numerous and far-flung the connections between them could be.

Garrison's embrace of nonresistant perfectionism both strengthened and eroded the Christian foundations of his abolitionist faith. In his own opinion, of course, perfectionism represented the Gospel's truest spirit and embodied a drive for ecclesiastical reformation that made it the direct extension of the great "come-outer" movements of Christian history, those led by Luther, Calvin, George Fox, John Huss, and of course the apostle Paul. For radical Hicksite Quakers like J. M. McKim, James Gibbon, Lucretia Mott, Arnold Buffum, and Angelina and Sarah Grimké, such thinking clearly approximated their own devotion to the "inner light" and suspicions of coercive authority, and they responded quickly to Garrison's latest call. So did contentious spiritual seekers, usually from dissenting religious backgrounds and humble New England origins, such as Parker Pillsbury, Stephen S. Foster, Abby Kelley, Nathaniel P. Rodgers, Charles Calistus Burleigh, and Henry C. Wright. Glimpsing boundless dreams of personal sanctification and driven by ceaselessly contentious energy, supporters of perfectionism such as these infused immediatism with a rich iconoclasm and an implacable hatred of compromise that did, quite literally, recall the Protestant Reformation.

But as Garrison assembled the congregation for his new religion, he also attracted adherents of a markedly more secular bent. In Boston, particularly where the influence of Unitarianism and of Harvard's intelligentsia held sway, militant abolitionism was often supported by a faith that closely equated the power of God with the rational workings of the human mind. To sophisticated and highly educated Brahmins such as Wendell Phillips, Edmund Quincy, Maria Weston Chapman, Anne and Deborah Weston, and Francis Jackson, Garrison's perfectionism seemed a refreshing denial of ossified traditions and promised to sweep away error, ignorance, and the dead weight of outdated religion, thereby inaugurating the era of vast social progress that God had foreordained for all His reasoning creations. Since these individuals too joined Garrison in castigating all compromise with the evils of church and government, Garrison never appreciated the clear deviations of their thinking from the pious traditions he so dearly prized. All that Garrison required was a wholesale refusal to comply with the demands of a corrupted nation, and Phillips, Quincy, Chapman, and the rest fulfilled that criteria easily.

By the fall of 1836, even before Garrison's meeting with Noyes, readers of the *Liberator* found themselves treated to samples of his new religious opinions, and some concluded that he had taken leave of his senses. Many of abolitionism's most powerful leaders recoiled instinctively at Garrison's thinking, and first among them were the men who ran the day-to-day business of the American Anti-Slavery Society in New York City. As the managers of mass mailings, petition drives, grass-roots agents, and the complex federation of state and local societies, Lewis Tappan, Henry B. Stanton, William Goodell, William Jay, Joshua Leavitt, and Elizur Wright, Jr. were deeply involved in the ongoing process of administering moral suasion. Garrison and his new supporters were, by contrast, much less involved in these complicated and constant managerial activities. Perhaps because of their commitments to these projects, the New York Tappanites disagreed deeply with Garrison's basic contention that the nation was unredeemably corrupt and believed very strongly that progress toward emancipation was actually being made. They pointed to the tens of thousands of ordinary citizens, suddenly sensitized by the abolitionists' agitations and the repression used to stop them, who now signed their petitions, bought their publications, and made strong statements of their own about the evils of the "slavepower." These people represented an enormous potential constituency, Tappanites believed, which needed to be drawn into the cause, not repulsed by irrelevant perfectionist heresies.

Garrison's doctrines themselves proved even more divisive than the tactical disagreements that they engendered. The plain fact was that Garrison's specific rejection of organized religion appeared as "rankest heresy" to stalwart evangelicals in every part of the movement, "undermining the whole fabric of social relations," as one of them put it. Likewise, to Birney, the Tappans, Elizur Wright and the rest, his antigovernment principles and personal refusal to vote seemed invitations to social chaos and exercises in political insanity. "I would to God that you could look at your late *Liberators* through my eyes," Elizur Wright, Jr. exclaimed bluntly, expressing well the feelings of so many of his colleagues. "*Bah*! I am sick of these outrages on God's common sense." As 1837 drew to a close and the wave of repression finally began to subside, Garrison had thus plunged the religion of immediatism into a protracted and disruptive reformation of its own, pitting dedicated but orthodox evangelical reformers such as the Tappans against committed visionaries and religious revolutionaries like himself. Over the next three years, he would come to regard as his mortal enemies not only the slaveholders, but also those among his fellow abolitionists who would, by destroying him, corrupt and undermine the crusading religion of immediate emancipation.

CHAPTER SEVEN

Reformation

Garrison first met the much-discussed Grimké sisters, Sarah and Angelina, in June 1837 when he invited them to New England for an extensive speaking tour. The Grimkés had been raised as southern belles outside of Charleston, South Carolina, but in young adulthood had rebelled against slavery. First Sarah and then Angelina chose to defy their plantation heritage by embracing the cause of immediate emancipation and fleeing to Philadelphia to join the Hicksite Quakers. Both were intelligent and outspoken, and Angelina blossomed into a superb public speaker. During 1836 each attempted to convert her homeland to immediatism, Angelina by publishing *An Appeal to the Christian Women of the South*, and Sarah her *Epistle to the Clergy of the South*, pamphlets which irate Charlestonians promptly burned. Garrison decided to put his close friend and fellow perfectionist Henry C. Wright in charge of the Grimkés' speaking itinerary, but as they traveled from town to town in Massachusetts it became clear that their advocacy of Garrison's religious "heresies" was becoming increasingly entangled with the issues of women's rights.

The Grimkés arrived in New England at a momentous juncture in the history of women's activism, which was finding important new sources of self-definition within the abolitionist crusade. In the early 1830s, when the movement had first begun, women from well-off evangelical households had joined enthusiastically, seeing the crusade as a means to promote human betterment while significantly extending their sphere of activity from the home into the public arena. At first they accepted without question the subordinate and separate roles to which their male colleagues assigned them as they circulated petitions, organized fundraising bazaars, and founded separate antislavery societies for females and "juveniles." In all these respects, their earliest activities paralleled the roles of women in any number of other benevolent causes, but by the time of the Grimkés arrival, this situation had begun to change. For one thing, abolitionist women learned as the decade passed that they were accomplishing a great deal in a very short time, especially in Massachusetts, and the statistics that described their work fostered feelings of pride and impatience. By 1837, the year the Grimkés appeared, the abolitionist women of Massachusetts had established nearly two hundred female and juvenile societies and had proven themselves at least as effective as men in raising funds and in circulating antislavery petitions. Equally important, powerful figures in Massachusetts such as Lydia Maria Child, Maria Weston Chapman, Anne Green Phillips, Mary Parker, Abby Kelley, and Deborah and Ann W. Weston began settling challenging examples for other women by earning significant reputations as speakers, writers, and organizers, confirming in so doing that their abilities often matched or exceeded those of their male colleagues.

All these developments greatly heightened the women abolitionists' sense that slavery had some disturbing connotations for their own subordinate status, and by 1837, with no encouragement from the Grimkés, they began voicing dissatisfaction openly. In that year, Massachusetts women took the lead in an attempt to create a national organization for women only, and during the course of their meeting many delegates agreed with Maria Weston Chapman's contention that, regarding the position of women in the movement, "things cannot remain as they are." Shortly thereafter, when the Grimkés arrived and started preaching women's rights along with antislavery, Massachusetts women were well prepared to join them in asking "what *then* can a woman do for a *slave* when she, herself, is under the feet of man and shamed into silence?"

In the beginning the Grimkés spoke only to small gatherings of women, but soon they began appearing before combined groups of both genders, "promiscuous assemblies" as detractors referred to them. As objections to this innovation by orthodox clerics and evangelicals began to surface, the Grimkés also made it clear that they were mixing perfectionism with their demands for women's rights, for Henry Wright had introduced them to the writings of John Humphrey Noyes. It was little wonder, then, that they found a strong ally when they finally met William Lloyd Garrison. "Dear Brother Garrison has been passing the day with us," Sarah reported, "and it has cheered my heart to find that he is fully with us on the subject of the rights of women." Angelina, on the same occasion, pressed Garrison to expand the *Liberator*'s editorial focus to include all the "grand principles" of "moral revolution," especially perfectionist nonresistance and women's rights, for "a new order of things is very desirable," she argued. "It is not only the cause of the slaves we plead, but the cause of women as moral, responsible beings."

The Grimkés' formulation of women's rights accorded easily with Garrison's emerging perfectionism and supported his own quests for independence and spiritual purity. Since his perfectionism already bespoke his deepening hostility to "illegitimate" authority, male domination over the political rights of women now seemed no less suspect to him than did Beecher's defense of the ordained clergy. The customs that denied women their freedom of expression in antislavery society meetings and prevented them from voting and holding offices as equals were coercive restrictions upheld by the unregenerate, preventing the movement from reflecting God's will. Of course the straightlaced Garrison felt no compulsion to follow this logic still further, as Noyes would soon do, to deny the moral legitimacy of civil marriages, or even of monogamy itself. Freedom of advocacy and political equality, never sexual revolution, were from the first the hallmarks of his feminism.

The history of Garrison's private relationships with women also disposed him favorably to the Grimkés' feminist appeals. Throughout childhood and adolescence, Fanny Garrison had held uncontested dominance over his development and even in her absence had kept him surrounded by other strong and demanding women. Preeminently the product of female influence, Garrison, as we have seen, came to adulthood regarding his innermost nature as timid, sentimental, and vulnerable, a view that the motherly Helen Garrison encouraged rather than challenged. The "lion-like" posture that Garrison struck in public always derived from his sense of his "womanish" inner self, as he himself referred to it, and from the very first he placed highest premium on the powers of women to inspire moral reform. Far too insecure to attempt to direct strong-willed women (his single effort having failed with Prudence Crandall) he instead deferred to them, believing that his feelings were closely tuned to theirs and that he would naturally concur with their points of view. And thanks, of course, to the patience of Helen Garrison, he never found cause in his life at home to inspect these assumptions critically.

By today's standards Garrison and the Grimké sisters' insistence on the rights of women to freedom of speech and access to the franchise might seem unremarkable enough. At the time, however, these demands, like immediate emancipation, proposed a fundamental reordering of political culture and human relations, and for this reason provoked deep-seated opposition. The 1820s and 1830s had witnessed an unprecedented expansion of political rights for white men, as politicians extended the franchise to all white males and new political parties actively sought their participation. The vote, in this respect, powerfully symbolized as never before males' dominion in shaping all phases of public life, even as the status of women was diminishing dramatically in law, politics, and in the workplace. In light of these circumstances, the sudden appearance of uncompromising female reformers who demanded equality inevitably touched off strong and widespread resistance, especially since they were supported by notorious firebrands like Garrison.

The first to attack Garrison's latest heresies was a group of orthodox evangelicals unaffiliated with the American Anti-Slavery Society, the General Association of Congregational Ministers, which sent a pastoral letter to all its congregations in August 1837. While not mentioning Garrison or the Grimkés by name, it did warn strongly against "dangers...which seem to threaten the female character with widespread and permanent injury" by "leading her to violate the modesty of her sex," and deplored those who denied the authority of ordained ministers. Only a week later, five more clergy, as professing abolitionists, issued a *Clerical Appeal* that accused Garrison by name of trafficking "in hasty, impious, almost ferocious denunciation" of the clergy, while promoting "intolerable departures from propriety by women." Next, the *New England Spectator*, editorial voice of Lyman Beecher and his followers, printed a long attack on Garrison by the highly regarded clergyman Levi Woodbury, who professed a zeal for abolitionism but no desire whatsoever to "swallow Garrison whole." The final orthodox remonstrance was the most impressive of all. Signed by the faculty of Andover Seminary, New England's leading evangelical center of learning, a *Second Clerical Appeal* stoutly defended male prerogatives, condemned perfectionism, and excoriated Garrison as the nation's most threatening moral disorganizer.

Garrison reprinted portions of each of these attacks in the "Refuge of Oppression," a front page column in the *Liberator* that he reserved each week for displaying the most extreme examples of proslavery thinking. Sensing correctly that New England's evangelical clergy were developing a concerted movement against him, he stoutly defended his perfectionism and the moral logic of women's rights, making it clear from the onset that he would never back down. "For my part, I am growing more and more irreverent and must be given over as incorrigible," he remarked wryly to Isaac Knapp. His personal attacks on the grievous moral failings of his critics, clergy and lay alike, grew even more extreme than his statements of doctrine, provoking shocked remonstrance on both grounds from

Tappanite members of the American Anti-Slavery Society. The first symptoms of a full-scale religious reformation, schisms in the ranks of the faithful, had now begun to appear.

Lewis Tappan, whose managerial temperament always led him to skirt around conflict, tried to rein in Garrison first by assuring the angry editor that he, too, deplored many parts of the *Clerical Appeals* and then by minimizing the significance of the issues raised. Yet Tappan also put it clearly to Garrison that he felt absolutely no sympathy for perfectionism, women's rights, or the *Liberator*'s vituperative attacks. The latter, especially, struck Tappan as wholly unwarranted and deeply harmful to the cause. The clerical dissenters, he argued, "come up to the average abolitionism of the day. By denouncing them, you denounce probably a majority of the members of the American Anti-Slavery Society. . . . We cannot afford to drive away friends who are substantially right." In a similar vein Birney privately lamented Garrison's behavior and censured it publicly in his own newspaper *The Philanthropist* but, unlike Tappan, he entertained "no exceptions that Mr. G. can be reduced to moderation." Neither did Henry Brewster Stanton, a firm Tappan ally who assessed the situation for Birney during an extended visit to Boston, considered by many to have become a Garrisonian stronghold. Most abolitionists in greater New England, he reported, sided with the writers of the *Clerical Appeals*, while "on the other hand, there is Garrison and his party, . . . resolutely bent on 'war to the knife and knife to the hilt.' " It was increasingly inevitable that evangelical abolitionists, some of them charter members of the American Anti-Slavery Society, would conclude with Birney that Garrison's departure from them might be "the best thing he could do for the cause of emancipation."

While Garrison's embrace of perfectionism and women's rights arose from his disillusionment with moral suasion in its original form, his vitriolic attacks on his newly emerging critics sprung from more complex motives. For over a decade he had struggled to square his thirst for fame and recognition with his quest for sanctification by defiantly asserting his moral independence. Now, as the decade of the 1830s entered its final years, he found himself in the paradoxical position of recognizing his own growing prominence in a nation he now believed to be more corrupt than ever. In this sense, the synthesis of his quest for success with the role of the prophet had, indeed, brought to him and his cause a significant measure of recognition. Conversely, any hint of compromise at this point would surely result in the collapse of his entire public career and with it all the hopes of black emancipation as well.

As controversy mounted with his fellow abolitionists, Garrison dwelled extensively on this thought in the *Liberator*, recalling how he had supposedly begun his abolitionist work unaided, or "a poor, self-educated mechanic—without important family connections, without wealth, without station." Though he had "stood alone," facing "trials, discouragements and perils" and opposed on all sides by church, state, and public opinion, his single-minded devotion to his uncompromised "independence," to "God and his truth and the rights of man," had always kept alive the promise of black emancipation. Had he listened to doubters who had warned him that his "principles and measures were wild and untenable," his power as a leader would have been destroyed and the slaves consigned to endless bondage. "The bark of abolition would have been wrecked upon the rocks...of human expedience." Since Garrison's personal fulfillment and the slaves' emancipation had always been synonymous in his mind, it now seemed all the more obvious to him that his personal acts of will must determine the course of history for the oppressed. The unwritten chapters of his own autobiography would be filled with fame and approbation, and those of the slaves with their glorious emancipation, if only he would persevere in upholding his independence:

I will not stop to trace the progress of this great enterprise. Suffice it to say, that its growth has been such as to astonish nations. Now, sir, if I possess any influence, it has been obtained by being utterly regardless of the opinions of mankind; if I have acquired any popularity, it has been owing to my sturdy unwillingness to seek that honor which comes from men; if I have been 'swallowed' by anybody, it is because I have always refused to 'confer with flesh and blood.' I have flattered no man, feared no man, bribed no man. Yet having made myself of no reputation, I have found a reputation; having refused to be guided by human opinions, I have won 'golden opinion' from the best of men; having sought that honor which comes from God, I am not left without honor among my countrymen.

Garrison always insisted to skeptical critics that he never proposed his new religious doctrines as tests for membership in the American Anti-Slavery Society. Time and again he emphasized that a belief in immediate uncompensated emancipation was all that should be required for good standing as an abolitionist, and that beyond this the "friends of the slaves" must remain as independent as he was, always free to differ on all other religious or moral questions. To do otherwise, he argued, ran counter to the original intentions of the founders of the American Anti-Slavery Society and violated principles of nonresistance that required full exercise of one's dictates of conscience. For these very reasons, he emphasized, he had always taken greatest pains to keep the *Liberator* editorially independent of all antislavery organizations: it always spoke only for him, never for any official society, when endorsing nonresistant perfectionism and condemning organized religion. And as for the "woman question," did not the *Declaration of Sentiments* of the American Anti-Slavery Society refer to "persons," not "men" when defining its membership, Garrison asked? Had not women been present at the meeting that founded the Society and had they not signed its *Declaration* as well?

It was his opponents, not he, Garrison always claimed, who were trying to impose new and coercive tests of membership, namely a belief in clerical authority, evangelical orthodoxy, and male supremacy. "Seditious plotters in our ranks," he charged, "open and avowed enemies" such as Elizur Wright, Jr., Birney, the Tappans, Stanton, William Goodell, and the rest, were fabricating novel definitions of abolitionist orthodoxy as part of a conspiracy to purge him and his supporters from the movement, while polluting the religion of immediatism with false and destructive doctrines. Certain that his enemies were now "busily engaged in holding caucuses, corresponding with each other and laying plots to carry their points against us," Garrison began mobilizing supporters of his own.

In charging his foes with conspiracy, Garrison was quite correct. By late 1837, all the leading Tappanites were engaging in extensive discussions about how best to bring Garrison to heel, or failing this, how to force him out of the movement. And from their perspective Garrison offered reasons aplenty for planning such a purge. Whatever his claims of speaking only for himself and not the American Anti-Slavery Society, the plain fact was that in the minds of most Americans Garrison's *Liberator* stood as the authoritative voice of the crusade against slavery. In the "market place of ideas" where Garrison traded so aggressively, his subtle arguments about his editorial independence counted for little compared to expressions of heretical beliefs that made potential converts recoil in dismay. Then too, Garrison's advocacy of women's rights was as personally offensive to his evangelical opponents as was his perfectionist anarchism, and just as repellant, they feared, to many who might otherwise sympathize with the cause. By 1837, it had become as clear to the Tappanites as it had to Garrison that many female abolitionists, not just the Grimkés, would no longer tolerate male co-workers who quoted the apostle Paul on female subservience while retaining all powers for themselves within the American Anti-Slavery Society. Foreseeing a feminist takeover of organizations which they felt they had built themselves, and threatened in general by feminist demands, Tappanite evangelicals ultimately drew the line at Garrison's endorsement of "promiscuous assemblies," agreeing wholeheartedly with Elizur Wright, Jr.'s contention that "Woman's Rights" was a "tin kettle" tied "to the tail of antislavery" and that the "tom turkeys," not the hens, "ought to do the gobbling."

And if Garrison's doctrines repelled his opponents, his supporters antagonized others as well. Some, like Wendell Phillips, Edmund Quincy, and Henry Chapman, were snobbish Boston blue bloods who haughtily dismissed as beneath contempt those who honestly attempted to engage them in disputes. Others, like Abby Kelley, Lucretia Mott, or the Grimkés, seemed to conduct themselves with a disquieting feminist militance or, like Maria Weston Chapman and her sisters, combined female strong-mindedness with insufferable aristocratic airs. Then there were those who seemed bewitched by eccentricity as well. Charles Calistius Burleigh sported cascading golden curls and clad himself in Old Testament prophet robes; Henry Clarke Wright claimed to remember his prenatal existence; and rough spoken rustics such as Parker Pillsbury, Stephen S. Foster, and Nathaniel Peabody Rodgers exceeded even Garrison in the use of vindicative language. To the Tappanites, these utopian dreamers, feminist cranks, and snobbish extremists suddenly seemed to be overrunning the movement.

Finally, there was the issue of Garrison himself, undoubtedly the most controversial personality of all to every participant in the emerging schism. To those who supported him, Garrison's overwhelming self-involvement and the intensity of his perfectionist vision seemed to make him a larger-than-life figure whose daring insights and inspiration dispelled their own ignorance, apathy, and reservations. Sensing in his prophesies rich new levels of meaning for their own lives, they shared a sense of gratitude to Garrison that only a lifetime of supporting him could ever repay. "How can we ever thank him for the clearing atmosphere to which he has lifted us," asked Wendell Phillips. To his supporters Garrison had indeed become a powerful liberator, a saint who had to be protected at all cost from those who sought his destruction. To his opponents, by contrast, the very same qualities revealed Garrison to be a monumentally self-centered tyrant and his followers mindless sycophants. To such critics, "the disgusting gross egotism of Garrison and the loathsome adulation of his admirers" were simply becoming unbearable. "I believe in my soul that we have all overvalued Garrison," wrote Gamaliel Bailey, a close associate of the Tappans, "and as to himself, pride has driven him mad." Amos Phelps, for his part, wrote bitterly that Garrison's "overgrown conceit had wrought him into the belief that his mighty self was abolition incarnate." Perhaps Theodore Weld put these conflicting assessments of Garrison's impact into their clearest perspective, shrewdly observing that "deep, irreconcilable *personal* animosities and repulsions" made hope for further cooperation among the abolitionists "utterly vain."

In late 1837, private animosities finally broke into open warfare when Garrison traveled to Worcester, Massachusetts, for the annual meeting of the Massachusetts Anti-Slavery Society. Stanton, Elizur Wright, Jr. and other clerical opponents were prepared to censure him there for his perfectionism and endorsements of women's rights but, as it turned out, Garrison and his supporters were equally well-prepared. John Gulliver, a close associate of the authors of the second *Clerical Appeal*, read a statement attacking Garrison for inexcusable egotism and religious heresy. The majority of the delegates, many of them women, immediately responded by dismissing Gulliver's complaints and expressing their total confidence in Garrison's leadership. They also made plain their conviction that neither perfectionism nor nonresistance represented doctrinal tests for membership in the Massachusetts Anti-Slavery Society, nor did the accident of one's particular gender. In his first trial of strength with his clerical opponents Garrison had won, cementing permanently his close alliance with the rapidly growing body of feminist abolitionists.

The sincerity of Garrison and his supporters in trying to separate nonresistance from the requirements of abolitionism soon became clear after the shocking murder of Elijah Lovejoy. In November 1837, this zealous abolitionist editor was gunned down by a mob in Alton, Illinois, after taking up arms in defense of his press. Lovejoy's recourse to violent means set off an

extended debate within the antislavery societies. Some dedicated pacifists like the Grimkés proposed that all immediatists
should be required to foreswear recourse to armed resistance in
response to physical attack, but Garrison firmly disagreed. Personally, he admitted, he greatly admired Lovejoy's bravery in
raising a gun to defend his freedom of expression, even though
as a nonresistant he could never condone the act of violence itself. But beyond this, he rejected the idea that the antislavery societies should require their members to practice pacifism in the
face of violent provocation: "If any man shall affirm that the antislavery cause...is answerable for our sentiments on this subject," he declared flatly, "to him may be justly applied the
apostolic injunction 'the truth is not in him.' " Abolitionists, he
stressed, must instead maintain what he termed a "broad platform" for the movement, where no extraneous criteria of religious doctrine or political creed would exclude the sincere
immediatist from full participation. His position was completely
consistent with his nonresistance principles, for he was rejecting
yet another form of godless coercion. But for opponents like
Henry B. Stanton and Elizur Wright, Jr. who had just been out-
voted in Worcester by Garrison's female supporters, such reassurance seemed transparently insincere. Garrison, in their view,
had already proven himself just as eager as any self-serving politician to manipulate resolutions and ballots in order to get his
way.

As they contested over doctrine within their movement, abolitionists everywhere also began to notice significant antislavery
trends emerging in northern politics, developments that politicians themselves in no way welcomed. The Whigs and the Democrats, the nation's two fiercely competitive political parties, had
maintained their organizations by creating powerful coalitions
of voters and interest groups that tied North and South together
in one well-developed structure of governance and power sharing. Each organization was closely managed by party chieftains
from both sections of the country, including such slaveholding
luminaries as John C. Calhoun, Andrew Jackson, Henry Clay,

and Alexander Stephens. Every politician knew perfectly well that open disagreements over slavery always caused these party allegiances to fracture ominously along sectional lines and were anxious, at all costs, to stifle all such disagreements. This tacit understanding, in part, had prompted President Jackson's efforts to legislate the abolitionists' suppression and had led the U.S. House of Representatives to enact its controversial gag rule forbidding the consideration of antislavery petitions. By the later 1830s, however, this ban on congressional debates over slavery had, in itself, become an issue that inflamed exactly such discussions, mobilizing northern voters for the first time to express their hostilities toward the slaveholding South.

The abolitionists themselves were greatly responsible for this portentous turn of events. Thanks to the grass-roots efforts of thousands of volunteers, the House of Representatives found itself by 1837 literally deluged with antislavery petitions bearing the signatures of hundreds of thousands of northerners, women as well as men. The gag rule constituted its official response, which in turn became the subject of unprecedented political dispute. Ex-President John Quincy Adams, now a Whig congressman from Massachusetts, objected vehemently and incessantly to this abridgement of the right of petitions and freedom of debate, and soon he was joined by a small but ever-growing group of northern Whig colleagues who in turn defied the gag rule by presenting petitions at every opportunity and generally agitated slavery questions in Congress at even the most irrelevant moments.

In this fashion, the self-propelling cycle of abolitionist agitation and officially sanctioned repression finally began creating groups of northern voters who insisted that their own elected representatives articulate their constituency's stern opposition to slaveholding, to violations of civil rights, and to the political behavior and social values of the planter class. None of these insurgent politicians was an immediate abolitionist, but all were eager to contest the morality of slavery regardless of party discipline, and their motives for speaking out only multiplied in the later 1830s after the independent Republic of Texas, an enormous slaveholding territory, petitioned Congress to be incorporated into the federal Union. As abolitionists divided over perfectionism, nonresistance, and women's rights, politicians in Washington opened disagreements of their own over the westward expansion of slavery, disagreements that would finally split the Union and lead to the Civil War.

To his opponents, these important political developments made Garrison's banishment from organized abolitionism all the more imperative. Thousands of conventional northerners, they now began to argue, were suddenly becoming sensitive to the sins of slavery, and it would be a tactical disaster to repel this political constituency with Garrisonian heresies like nonresistance and women's rights. To Garrison's sharpest critics, moral suasion finally seemed to be succeeding by reaching an ever-larger number of ordinary voters, voters who now must be challenged by fully committed abolitionists to direct their political energies toward achieving immediate emancipation. To Leavitt, Birney, Simeon Jocelyn, Goodell, Myron Holley, and other anti-Garrisonians, organized political action now seemed a compelling way to convert political antislavery into nationally legislated emancipation, while at the same time completely banishing the feminist abolitionists through a reliance on the male-only franchise. Soon these leaders began insisting that all right-thinking abolitionists must make it their duty to cast their ballots for political candidates opposed to slavery. Some even contemplated the formation of a totally new political party pledged to immediate emancipation that would challenge the electorate on every ballot to cast their votes for antislavery candidates.

Of all the proposals of his most zealous opponents, none struck harder at everything that Garrison stood for than did the idea that abolitionists must be required to become voters. Such a rule represented a wholesale assault on his cherished sense of independence, his nonresistants' refusal to acknowledge coercive laws, his insistence that women be made the political equals of men, and his perfectionist drive to sanctify himself by transcending corrupting institutions. He had also concluded long ago, from bitter experiences as a Federalist party editor, that practicing political journalism meant being enslaved to the fickle and worldly tastes of a partisan readership. To encumber his mandate as the *Liberator's* guiding spirit with a partisan political mission was to subvert every moment of self-emancipation he had ever achieved, to forfeit all his power to continue as the prophet-visionary of abolitionism, and to abandon his dreams of personal success, fame, and sanctification through the achievement of black emancipation. Political abolitionism, in short, proposed the utter destruction of Garrison's religion of immediate emancipation. It is little wonder that he regarded it, from the first, as the most heinous maneuver of all those undertaken by his godless opponents.

In midsummer 1838, Garrison launched a wholesale retaliation by announcing in the *Liberator* that he was proposing to establish a Non-Resistance Society. Since Birney, Goodell, Leavitt, and their followers were now insisting that political voting must be required of all abolitionists, Garrison reasoned that a nonresistance movement must oppose such coercive schemes, but it must do so in a manner consistent with perfectionism by remaining entirely separate from the rules or structures of the American Anti-Slavery Society. Henry C. Wright, Abby Kelley, John Collins, Samuel J. May, and Edmund Quincy, his closest nonresistance associates, now began lining up delegates for the meeting that would found the New England Non-Resistance Society. By attempting to maintain this rigorous separation between abolitionism and nonresistance, Garrison's consistent support for the necessity of maintaining the broad platform of the American Anti-Slavery Society could not have been clearer. No less clear was his opponents' intention to encumber that platform with novel and restrictive tests that they well knew Garrison could never accept.

The meeting itself took place in Boston's Marlboro Chapel on September 18, 1838, and attracted 160 delegates, many of them perfectionist Garrisonians. Some, like Wendell Phillips, were certainly not pacifists but wished to register their strong support for Garrison in the ever-expanding struggle against his conspiring foes. After Abby Kelley was voted a place on the business committee and while the convention was rejecting both capital punishment and all war between nations, Garrison wrote a *Declaration of Sentiments* for the Non-Resistance Society. "Never was a more 'fanatical' or 'disorganizing' instrument penned by man," he boasted, and indeed his statement hurled a wholesale challenge against not only political abolitionism, but against all claims to obedience by any secular authority:

> As every human government is upheld by physical strength, and its laws are enforced virtually at the point of the bayonet, we cannot hold any office which imposes upon its incumbent the obligation to compel men to do right, on pain of imprisonment or death. We therefore voluntarily exclude ourselves from every legislative and judicial body, and repudiate all human politics, worldly honors, and stations of authority. If we cannot occupy a seat in the legislature or on the bench, neither can we elect others to act as our substitutes in any such capacity.

"Physical coercion," the *Declaration* continued, was "not adapted to moral regeneration." Since humanity's "sinful disposition can be subdued only by love," all true government must be based exclusively on an "allegiance to *Him* who is *King of Kings* and *Lord of Lords*."

Though only 25 of the original 160 delegates finally signed this extreme formulation of perfectionism and nonresistance, those who did were now well-situated to help Garrison promote perfectionism outside the American Anti-Slavery Society, even as they battled the heretics who wished to transform it into what he termed a "soulless engine of party politics." The Non-Resistance Society would have only a brief and lackluster future, but for now it bound his supporters together in an insurgent and soul-inspired fellowship prepared to battle with noncoercive weapons of perfectionism for the integrity of the emancipationist creed. "Our association," he wrote, "places every man on the dead level of equality. He that would be the greatest must be the servant of all. It gives no power but that of love, and allows nothing but suffering for Christ's sake."

His assurance of self-purity thus fortified, Garrison was eager to employ any strategy that would insure his ongoing control of the American Anti-Slavery Society. In his zeal to reform the membership of the immediatist organization, he had now established the separate Non-Resistance Society, and in this respect Elizur Wright, Jr. made good sense when complaining to Garrison that "the deceitful spirit of sect" had "stolen upon you unaware, and that you are becoming...a *close communion anti-sectarianist*." Garrison's sincere claims of devotion to the noncoercive, broad abolitionist platform notwithstanding, he could tolerate no deviation from emancipationist orthodoxy as he now understood it.

While Garrison rallied the forces of perfectionism, Henry B. Stanton led an attempt to capture Massachusetts for political abolitionism. In local meetings throughout the state in late 1838, anti-Garrisonian delegates presented numerous resolutions declaring it the duty of every abolitionist "not to content himself with merely refusing to vote for any man who is opposed to emancipation...but to throw his vote for some man known to favor it." Other motions bound abolitionists to campaign against proslavery political candidates, and one called for the creation of an officially sponsored newspaper, an antidote to the *Liberator*, that would urge abolitionists, as duty bound, to use their political as well as their moral and religious power "for the immediate overthrow of slavery." The 1839 annual meeting of the Massachusetts Anti-Slavery Society, which all these resolutions anticipated, promised a full-scale confrontation between Garrison and his antagonists, and in the *Liberator* he sounded the call to battle: "Give out a new watchword—so that there will be a general rallying of our early, intrepid, storm-proof, scarred veteran coadjutors ...proposed to give battle to internal contrivers of mischief."

As the meeting opened in Boston, Garrison's forces were clearly in control, thanks primarily to the sizeable participation of Boston's free African Americans and Massachusetts's female abolitionists. Though he knew he could command the support he needed to dictate the course of the meeting simply by moving that women be allowed to vote, Garrison showed his consistent regard for freedom of discussion by encouraging a free-wheeling debate. In attendance were nearly all of his most important opponents, and he gave them ample opportunity to air all their grievances against him. Stanton, for example, delivered a lengthy attack on perfectionism's blighting impact on the cause and censored the *Liberator* for its heresies. Charles T. Torrey, a prominent Tappanite, then suggested that the Society needed to create a new abolitionist newspaper devoted to political action, one that would be edited by someone with credentials matching those of Elizur Wright, Jr., or perhaps Stanton. Next, Stanton directly confronted Garrison on the political implications of nonresistance: "Mr. Garrison! do you or do you not believe it is a sin to go to the polls?" Abiding by his principles and therefore unwilling to make either voting *or* nonvoting a coercive test of abolitionist credentials, Garrison replied simply, "Sin for *me*," and suddenly May, Phillips, and Henry C. Wright began flying to Garrison's defense.

When the first item of business was finally brought to the floor and President Francis Jackson, a strong Garrison supporter, ruled it *"in order for women to vote,"* all could see who really controlled the Massachusetts Anti-Slavery Society. Resolutions requiring voting on the part of abolitionists were crushed, 180–24, with women supplying a powerful number of "nays." Afterward Stanton angrily wrote Birney that Garrison "with his trained bands, . . . made a desperate push to sway the Society over to his nonresistance views. He succeeded." More accurately, Stanton and his friends had tried to make political action and the suppression of women's rights into articles of faith in a new abolitionist orthodoxy, and they had failed. But whatever one's explanations Stanton was certainly correct when observing that "the split is wide open and can never be closed up."

Meanwhile, at the American Anti-Slavery Society's headquarters in New York City, Lewis Tappan grew increasingly disillusioned with the developments in Massachusetts. Lamenting his involvement with Garrison as a "sad mistake," he was equally unhappy with Stanton's zeal for party politics. By 1839, however, these were only two of the many interrelated problems that bedeviled Tappan and the national organization. Foremost among these was a crippling loss of revenue caused by the financial depression that had begun in 1837. In addition, the national society's grass roots support had begun to disappear, in part the result of the petition campaign which placed great stress on local and highly decentralized activism, moving the focus of authority away from the American Anti-Slavery Society. Just as harmful, however, was Garrison's personal influence, since many local churches were repelled by his doctrines and retreated from the cause by cutting off donations. Strapped for funds, state societies then withdrew agents from the field and began squabbling among themselves over finances as well as doctrines.

As the organizational substructure of the American Anti-Slavery Society began to collapse, Stanton, Birney, and others hastened the process by seceding from the Massachusetts Anti-Slavery Society in 1839. Concluding that Garrison had now achieved a stranglehold over that body, they turned in their memberships and by May had established their own Massachusetts Abolition Society on the explicit principles of compulsory voting, male supremacy, and church-centered evangelicalism. Disputes over the status of this new organization relative to the national Society in New York grew endlessly tangled and were deeply divisive. At the same time, letters flew between Myron Holley, James G. Birney, Joshua Leavitt, and Henry B. Stanton touting the idea of establishing a separate abolitionist political party, a proposal that Lewis Tappan, Theodore Weld, and Gamaliel Bailey deeply opposed. Garrison's opponents were now dividing over the meanings of political action even as they rallied to purge him from the movement.

In this atmosphere rife with rancor and suspicion, everyone knew that a permanent schism was inevitable when the American Anti-Slavery Society convened in New York City for its annual meeting in May 1840. Preparing for that confrontation, the apostles of political action met in Albany, New York, to form the Liberty party, nominating James G. Birney for President of the United States in the election of 1840 and directly challenging both Garrison's creed and the nations's system of two-party politics. Garrison, in response, published *An Address to the Abolitionists of the United States*, which condemned the Liberty party as a fatally corrupt capitulation to an "unregenerate" political system. The party was doomed to fail because its creators, after all, were proving themselves to be "irresponsible individuals" who were eager to barter the fates of three million slaves for "the loaves and fishes of political preferment." As he prepared to leave for the annual meeting, Garrison predicted "a desperate struggle" and "the breakup of our whole organization," but his mind, he wrote, was "calm and peaceful." Contributing to his sense of serenity was surely the knowledge that his agents had been criss-crossing the North for months to line up delegates, and that he had arranged discount railway and steamship tickets for New York City–bound loyalists who might be low on funds. Both sides were working hard to pack the meeting, but Garrison, the great foe of politics, turned out to be the superior organizer.

When the annual meeting finally convened on May 12, its outcome was settled on the very first vote when Presiding Officer Francis Jackson placed Abby Kelley on the Business Committee. Birney objected and when his dissenting motion failed, 557–451, he was joined by Stanton and Lewis Tappan in withdrawing from the committee on the explicit grounds of male supremacy. They declared in their statement of resignation that the innovations seemed "repugnant to the Constitution of the

Society—that it was throwing a firebrand into anti-slavery meetings—that it was contrary to the usages of the civilized world—that it tended to destroy the efficacy of female antislavery activity." Soon thereafter, nearly three hundred dissenters officially seceded from the American Anti-Slavery Society to form the American and Foreign Anti-Slavery Society, managed by an all-male executive committee and supported by a "Women's Auxiliary." The issues of gender in conjunction with religious and political controversies had proven sufficiently divisive to fracture permanently the American Anti-Slavery Society.

Garrison now presided over a truncated but far more harmonious American Anti-Slavery Society, the "old organization" as its members now began calling it. They promptly elected Lucretia Mott, Maria Weston Chapman, and Lydia Maria Child to the executive committee and roundly denounced the Liberty party and the American and Foreign Anti-Slavery Society. No one, however, even suggested the idea of making nonresistant perfectionism or any other of Garrison's personal beliefs into new tests of membership. Once in control, Garrisonians remained as faithful as ever to the liberating principles of the broad platform. "We have made clean work of everything," Garrison reported proudly to Helen—"adopted thoroughgoing resolutions—and taken the strongest ground—with *crashing* unanimity." With the heretics purged and the abolitionist fellowship reformed, the religion of immediatism and the organization of the American Anti-Slavery Society were again as one, with Garrison assured his independent role of inspired visionary and denunciatory prophet.

Debate continues to this day as to which group of abolitionists, Garrison or his critics, adopted the wiser approach for opposing slavery after the schism of 1840. There is much to be said for James G. Birney's contention that Americans needed the "tangible means" that only the ballot could offer to make their opposition to slavery affect the course of public events. In a nation governed by its passion for politics, the act of voting, he argued, truly did mean exercising the levers of power in a morally consistent fashion, and this was in actuality how, in his opinion, substantial reform could be achieved. How many Americans, he wondered, would ever be moved to action by Garrison's perverse reversal of this political theorem—that the best way to work for emancipation was to "sit on one's hands" by consciously choosing *not* to vote? The answer to his question would become obvious over the next two decades since nonvoting Garrisonians would always remain a tiny minority, even as the power of antislavery grew ever stronger in electoral politics.

Nevertheless, Garrison was profoundly correct, and disturbingly so, when admonishing his apostate colleagues that slavery and racism could never be truly obliterated without a previous revolution in the moral values of all white Americans, voters included. Antislavery politicians, he always warned, would inevitably succumb to compromise with the system of coercion and corruption from which they had arisen; winning elections would take precedence over freeing slaves, not only in the minds of elected officials but in the hearts of the voters who put them in office. And if, by chance, emancipation did result through the votes of the "unregenerate," race prejudice would persist as strongly as ever and would turn the promise of black freedom into a cruel hoax. The next two decades of national struggle over slavery and the terrible war that followed would finally begin to determine whether Birney or Garrison was the wiser visionary.

CHAPTER EIGHT

Disunion

Fresh from his triumphs within the American Anti-Slavery Society, Garrison sailed straightway for London in May 1840, where British collaborators were convening the World Anti-Slavery Convention. He knew that some of his leading American opponents, namely, Birney, Stanton, and Gerrit Smith, were already busy there, discrediting heretical "Garrisonism" and justifying themselves as faithful embodiments of the immediatist creed. It worried him, too, that the British invitation had already stressed to Americans that "gentlemen only were expected to attend," a sure sign that his powerful overseas allies were being swayed by his most dangerous domestic opponents.

Anticipating an extension of the victories he had just concluded against the new organization, Garrison assembled a formidable delegation to join him in representing the American Anti-Slavery Society—feminists Lucretia Mott, Maria Weston Chapman, and Ann Greene Phillips, the talented African American Charles Lennox Remond, and two of his most impressive white male associates, Wendell Phillips and Nathaniel P. Rodgers. On his first trip to England in 1833, Garrison recalled, a public confrontation with his American opponents had yielded him one of his greatest triumphs in the discrediting of the American Colonization Society, not to mention his own emergence as undisputed leader in the global struggle against slavery. Now history would surely repeat itself, as Garrison and his fellow delegates exposed the new organization to British abolitionists for the "godless conspiracy" against black freedom that it really was. Birney and the rest would return to the United States in disgrace. Garrison, vindicated, would enjoy once more the plaudits of British admirers. History failed dismally to follow his expectations, however, revealing instead that his recent victory over the new organization was creating as many problems as it solved.

The World Anti-Slavery Convention opened in London the day before Garrison arrived and as its first order of business dealt him and his supporters a serious reversal. Wendell Phillips had attempted to amend the rules that prohibited women from voting as delegates, the very same tactic that Garrison himself had recently employed to exert control over the Anti-Slavery Society. This time, however, the maneuver failed completely, for defenders of male prerogatives from both sides of the Atlantic united in striking down Phillips's motion. When Garrison finally arrived the following day he elected to join the rejected women in the balcony in silent protest, and all the Garrisonians boycotted the proceedings.

In the aftermath of the convention, Garrison unfairly suggested to Helen that Phillips had mishandled the "woman question," and that "we would have carried the point triumphantly" had he, Garrison, only arrived in time to lead the fight. But in so alleging, Garrison was really registering his deep concern over this humiliating reversal and its implications. As the World Convention indisputably revealed, his latest formulation of reform theology—perfectionism, nonresistance and women's rights—did not compel the automatic assent that the slogans of immediatism once had, and neither did his claim as a prophetic leader of nonresistant perfectionism. Anxious as always to be recognized as foremost in a righteous and despised minority, Garrison now had grounds for fearing that his stature within that vanguard was suddenly lessening perceptibly, and that the heroic spirit of the 1830s was starting to flag.

In retrospect, the reasons for this sudden erosion of Garrison's public position were obvious. For one thing, Birney, Leavitt, and the rest of his abolitionist enemies did not personify

those discredited programs that had once made the colonizationist leaders such easy prey. By 1840, these opponents had
earned credentials as reforming editors, courageous martyrs,
and moral agitators in their own right, and Garrison could no
longer claim for himself any monopoly of abolitionist leadership. In addition, the political abolitionists seemed to be proposing an innovative, straightforward approach to emancipation
that accorded quite well with both the British experience of legislated emancipation and with the American infatuation with
politics. Their insistence on upholding male prerogatives and
ministerial authority also matched the preferences of most British reformers, just as it appealed to most American males. Garrison, by contrast, now seemed to many to have embraced a
disturbing mélange of causes that were hard to explain, lacked
coherence, and had no self-evident pertinence to the specific
goal of ending black slavery. In the free marketplace of ideas
Garrison now found himself attempting to sell a multitude of
doctrines that were inestimably more difficult to explain than
the simple, clarion call for immediate emancipation. In the immediate aftermath of the schism in the American Anti-Slavery
Society, Garrison had boasted that he and his supporters "now
head the hosts of freedom." But six months after that climactic
event, the euphoria of victory had given way to disturbing uncertainty. Garrison now had good reason to worry that he was in
danger of losing not only his audience but also his claim of being abolitionism's peerless moral prophet.

   Returning to Boston in mid-August 1840, Garrison did his
best to strike a confident public pose, even as he complained in
private "of the introduction of the new organization spirit in
England." He assured his *Liberator* readers that his mission in
the British Isles had constituted "one of the most important
movements of my life" and that his boycott of the London convention had opened the eyes of backward Europeans to the
cause of women's rights. Despite this brave front, however, he
could mask neither his chagrin over his disappointing reception

in England nor a mounting concern over his future. Setting
aside for a rare moment his abiding hostility to dominant American values, he bluntly proclaimed to friends who had gathered
for his homecoming reception that "I thank God I was born in
the United States and that my field of labor lies in the United
States." Many of the English abolitionists whose esteem he had
once fervently courted had now gone soft, he declared in the
Liberator, infected "with proslavery delicacy and feeling" and incapable of the moral vision available only to mob-seasoned
American immediatists. The true "friends of the bondsmen,"
meaning the sanctified membership of the American Anti-
Slavery Society, now had no choice but to commence their agitations anew, facing "former friends, now sworn enemies, both at
home and, alas, abroad."

The plain fact was, however, that the American Anti-Slavery
Society no longer possessed resources to support these brave
words, transacting only a small fraction of its former business.
Its newspaper, the *National Anti-Slavery Standard*, existed on meager funding that left it never far from bankruptcy. The annual
meetings in New York City often failed to attract a respectable
number of delegates, since most of the state auxiliaries were
moribund or had withdrawn their allegiances during the recent
schism. Only the Massachusetts Anti-Slavery Society maintained a well-run network of Garrisonian agencies, although
smaller outposts of supporters remained active in Ohio, Pennsylvania, western New York state and New Hampshire. Few if any
funds came to the national office from these remaining sources. Petition campaigns had to cease, and antislavery agents were dropped
from the payroll. In desperation, Garrison even dispatched his
close friend John A. Collins on a fruitless mission back to England
to solicit funds from the few abolitionists there still loyal to the old
organization. "We are really in a more critical situation than we
have ever been in before," Garrison fretted, "and unless we can get
some aid from abroad, I am apprehensive that the American Anti-
Slavery Society, with the *Standard*, must sink."

Compounding the problem of finances was "the political excitement now raging like a whirlwind in the country." The presidential election of 1840 developed into the most hotly contested of any in American history until that time, and it was clear that most abolitionists were as eager as any other group of voters to participate. They disregarded in impressive numbers the Garrisonian warning that the act of voting meant a compromise with slavery. Embarrassingly, even some of Garrison's most prominent supporters—George Bradburn, David Lee Child, Ellis Gray Loring and Samuel Sewall—publicly supported the Whig party on the grounds that, in Massachusetts at least, Whigs were more receptive to abolitionism than were Democrats. "A large proportion of the abolitionists," Garrison admitted, were "determined to go with their party at the approaching election, and they will not attend our meetings until after the election, if at all." His denouncing editorials against all voting, and especially against the politics of the Liberty party, did nothing to slow the trend. William Henry Harrison, the Whig nominee, captured the presidency with abolition-minded voters supporting him almost unanimously. Garrison could take solace only in the fact that the Liberty party's performance proved just as irrelevant to the political process as his own, with Birney polling a paltry 7,069 votes. Although the Liberty party's prospects were soon to brighten, nationally organized abolitionism was now collapsing, and so, it seemed, was Garrison's standing as America's leading immediatist.

Pressed by powerful political competitors and worried over shrinking resources, Garrison surprised his allies and opponents alike by putting forth a startlingly new announcement in early 1842, declaring that the North must peacefully secede from the South. This shocking new demand that there be "NO UNION WITH SLAVEHOLDERS" was a logical extension of his perfectionism. But it also spoke directly to his concern that electoral politics had done much to undermine moral suasion. The Liberty party, which Garrison so despised, and the American voter, who had so resolutely ignored his denunciation of balloting, had both certainly given Garrison reason to reject the United States Constitution. By 1843, the Liberty party had established strong organizations in Ohio, Pennsylvania, and especially in Garrison's Massachusetts, where members exerted indisputable influence in state elections by urging the electorate to forsake its corrupt allegiances to the Whig and Deomcratic parties and to vote instead for candidates pledged to ending slavery. To the consternation of slaveholding politicians, portions of the northern Whig party, in response, also began presenting themselves as supporters of freedom, promising to resist annexation of the slaveholding Republic of Texas, to repeal the gag rule, and to end all support for slavery on the part of the federal government.

Powerful competitors were now seizing the initiative from Garrison in the expanding political struggle against slavery, and his answer was equally political—declaring that the Constitution of the United States represented a "Covenant with Death, An Agreement With Hell" from which all abolitionists must nonviolently withdraw their allegiance. To prove his contentions, he reminded his readers that the Founding Fathers had counted the slave as three-fifths of a person for determining representation and taxation, had obligated national authorities to suppress slave insurrections, and had made provision for the nation's capital to reside in a slave society. All of these measures, he argued, secured for slaveholding interests the formidable power of the federal government. According to Garrison, the only real choice left to God-fearing abolitionists was to sever all moral allegiances to the Union by refusing to vote, to hold office, or to swear civil oaths to the federal government. Just as perfectionist Christians must cast off all ties to coercive religion, so must righteous abolitionists peaceably remove themselves from supporting in any way the politics or government of a proslavery nation.

Judged in light of these truths, Garrison argued, the Liberty party represented a hopeless but still dangerous experiment. Instead of demanding that "*the people be brought to repentance*," Birney and the rest were proposing to dupe honest citizens into becoming corrupted voters whose attempts to cast ballots for freedom would only leave them compromising with oppression. Just as reprehensible, the Liberty party also accustomed its supporters "to the love of political preferment rather than the duty of Christian reformation," and what held true for the Liberty party also applied to Whigs and Democrats, since voting for any party could never substitute for moral suasion: "The only reason why the two great political parties are not anti-slavery is because the people of the land are proslavery," Garrison insisted. "Political action is not moral action any more than a box on the ear is an argument," since spiritual reformation, not election results, was "the mode appointed by God to conquer error and destroy the works of darkness." By personally withdrawing all allegiances to the federal Union and by arming themselves with cry of "No Union with Slaveholders," true abolitionists must oppose all these godless trends, appealing beyond the hollow rituals of balloting to challenge the corrupted structure of the nation's government and the complicity of all whose votes supported it.

To Garrison, the new disunionist creed always embodied a redoubled assertion of the first principles of moral suasion, dating from 1830, from which Liberty men and "new organizationists" had so badly strayed. While third-party abolitionists strove to make their doctrines popular, supposedly judging their success by the number of voters they commanded, Garrison and his fellow disunionists would persevere as a despised minority devoted exclusively to truth. (Did Jesus of Nazareth care how many voted for him? Garrison liked to ask.) In this sense, the cry for "No Union with Slaveholders" now served for Garrison as a literal extension of immediate emancipation, for like immediatism, disunionism rejected all equivocation, left no room for compromise, scoffed at reliance on step-by-step solutions, and scorned the precedents of tradition. Like immediatism, moreover, it offered no structured plan for solving the problem of slavery, insisting only that slavery would never end until all Americans united in spirit to denounce it. And like immediatism, "No Union with Slaveholders" furnished its zealous adherents with a highly disturbing demand that questioned the legitimacy of the dominant trends of the era. In the 1830s, the first generation of immediate abolitionists had confronted a society stirred to a new sense of piety by evangelical revivalism. In the 1840s disunionists hoped to do likewise, challenging a nation preoccupied by politics but increasingly divided by sectional tension over slavery's possible expansion.

In short, the doctrine of northern disunion offered Garrison the chance to reassert his accustomed role. For over a decade he had pursued his calling by scorning corruption and issuing clarion cries for individual repentance, insisting that "moral revolution" alone would free the slaves. In this respect the demand for "No Union with Slaveholders," like immediatism, supported perfectly his abiding hatred of unregulated passion, distrust of conventional sources of power, his longstanding quest for personal holiness and fame, and his exacting equation between his own anticipated vindication and the millennial moment of the slaves' emancipation. And like immediatism, espousals of disunion allowed Garrison to envision himself once more as the nation's unmatched moral prophet, armed with a God-given truth so all-embracing that only the most sanctified could dare espouse it while facing the jeers of a fallen world:

> We shall be ridiculed as fools, scorned as visionaries, branded as disorganizers, reviled as madmen, threatened, and perhaps punished as traitors. But we shall bide our time....Our faith in God is rational and steadfast. We have exceeding great and precious promises on which to rely, that *we are in the right*.

Believing, as always, that he could make the future conform to his prophesies, Garrison quickly set out to make the doctrine of northern disunionism the centerpiece of the abolitionist creed.

Once again, however, the future failed notably to follow Garrison's bidding, for even the most faithful were initially unwilling to enroll in his new crusade. When he first broached disunionism at the 1842 meeting of the American Anti-Slavery

Society, the delegates refused even to entertain it as suitable for the agenda. In its next annual meeting in 1843, the national organization found itself in such fiscal disarray that Garrison's disunion resolution was tabled in favor of heated debates as to whether or not the Society itself should disband, move to Boston in order to save money, or continue to limp along in New York City. When it was finally agreed that the nominal headquarters would remain in New York, but the Executive Committee could transact its business from Boston, one fact was clear. Whatever the Anti-Slavery Society's ultimate view of disunion, its action would carry no institutional significance whatever for the conduct of American politics. Though in 1843 Garrison did succeed in securing the passage of disunionist resolutions in the Massachusetts Anti-Slavery Society, it was not until 1844 that "No Union with Slaveholders" finally became the motto on the banner of the American Anti-Slavery Society. The vote 59–21 measured well not only the significant proportion of disunionsim's opponents, but also the paltry number that still bothered to attend the society's meetings. Measured by these standards, Garrison's hopes for inspiring a revitalized crusade to revolutionize a fallen nation had already died aborning. A host of talented supporters of long standing such as David Lee and Lydia Maria Child, Amasa Walker, Arnold Buffum, James A. Gibbon, Ellis Gray Loring, and George Bradburn canceled their memberships. So did unknown numbers of those less famous.

Garrison now found himself presiding over a shrinking and ever more tightly knit gathering of saints. While the Garrisonian disunionists remained no less combative and radical a movement than abolitionism had ever been, theirs also became an increasingly self-contained community during the 1840s. Its center was Boston, where its most powerful organizers resided, and soon both critics and members began referring to the group as "the Boston clique." Leaders included, besides Garrison, such men and women of privilege, education, taste, and distinguished lineage as Wendell Phillips, Edmund Quincy, Francis Jackson, Samuel J. May, the Weston sisters Deborah and Ann, and Maria Weston Chapman. Following the decision to permit the Executive Committee to transact its business in Boston, these "select few of us" (as Phillips referred to them) managed among themselves all the important business of the American Anti-Slavery Society and acted as the definitive doctrinal arbiters of disunionist abolitionism.

Immensely secure in their own social position and committed to the noncoercive principles of free expression, these aristocrats gladly embraced in their fellowship a raucous group of perfectionist agitators of humble circumstances such as Henry C. Wright, John A. Collins, Charles C. Burleigh, Abby Kelley Foster and Stephen S. Foster, Parker Pillsbury, and Nathaniel Peabody Rodgers. Sharing a deep estrangement from the nation that continuously scorned their calls for moral revolution, the members of the clique drew inspiration to continue their arduous crusade by supporting one another as an extended family, "a world in ourselves and each other," as Deborah Weston defined it. Members of the clique named their children after one another, shared meals, officiated at the weddings of one another's children, organized fundraising events, relieved the financial stress of poorer colleagues, and performed many other day-to-day rituals that bound them together in a warm and intimate gathering of saints.

For the first time in his life, perhaps, Garrison began to flourish emotionally within this vibrant community. Making few distinctions between his own personal family and the dear friends who surrounded him, he sometimes characterized both groups as one, his "little band," and named two of his children after cherished comrades Francis Jackson and Wendell Phillips (three others he named after British abolitionists). As with the members of his natural family, he generally addressed clique members in deeply supportive terms of "brotherhood" and "sisterhood." Moreover, he consciously fostered a spirit of free discussion among his colleagues with a patience, humor, and candor that reassured his colleagues, allowing all to feel that their individual views were truly respected. "I think Garrison has done his work wisely and well," observed Ann Weston to Wendell Phillips, for within the clique everyone trusted that "there might be honest differences of opinion." Reciprocating in kind, his colleagues, rich and humble alike, always made it clear to Garrison that they regarded him as a very special and much-revered family member, honoring him as their "Father Garrison," the prophet who had entered each of their lives as God's inspired instrument. Edmund Quincy, for example, believed that Garrison was "one of those rare spirits which Heaven, at distant periods, sends upon the earth on holiest missions," while to Samuel J. May, Garrison's "genius" had given "a new conception of the majesty and power of a single human life." Though sometimes critical of his personal quirks and over-zealous tendencies, they nevertheless looked to him as their mentor, praising his faultless moral judgment, turning to him to solve their personal squabbles, and relying on him to maintain noncoercive personal dynamics within the group itself. Garrison, for his part, made clear time and again his eagerness "to take the advice of (his) friends" and his "desire that it be given without reserve."

Garrison, in short, was finally surrounding himself with the nurturing family that he had always been denied. Committed in public to defiant postures of unconquerable independence, he now received reassurance within the clique that he would no longer need to face hostility or financial adversity alone. While friends reassured him of their loyalty and love, Phillips, Quincy, and Jackson supplemented his household budget, kept track of the finances of the *Liberator*, and even absorbed his larger expenses such as college tuition and rent. "Were it within my power do to so," Samuel J. May once wrote him, "I would raise you up on a cloud of air, fly you away to the lands of your dreams and take from you all your cares." As he absorbed the support that others so generously offered, he responded in kind, enjoying in private a rich measure of the acceptance and respect for which he still hungered in public.

Meanwhile, Garrison's responsibilities with his natural family also began compounding. Helen and Lloyd's first child, a son named George Thompson Garrison, had arrived in 1836, and a rapid succession of children had soon followed. William was born in 1838 and Wendell two years later. By 1842 another son, Charles Follen, had arrived, followed in two years by their first daughter Fanny, named for Garrison's mother. Elizabeth Pease was born in 1844, and in 1848 the family was completed with the birth of Francis Jackson. Elizabeth, always sickly, lived only two years while Charles, at seven, died of complications from an accidental scalding administered by his father in a tragic effort to battle rheumatic fever. Garrison was at once an enthusiastic and energetic father, giving to his children the paternal affection that his own childhood had so lacked by organizing family outings and by always being ready for games, storytelling, songfests, and practical jokes. Applying abolitionist principles to the nurturing of his children, he sent them all to racially integrated schools and reared them carefully in the religious doctrine of nonresistant immediatism. Searching for more ample quarters, the family moved several times during the 1840s, but always continued to welcome an endless succession of visiting relatives and clique friends. Though "never so far in funds as to have a spare dollar," guests often helped supplement the household budget of his "abolitionist hotel," and these donations were gratefully accepted.

As the decade of the 1840s advanced, Garrison's domestic affairs were complicated still further by the unexpected return of his long-lost brother, James. After twenty terrible years at sea, James suddenly appeared in Boston, physically and emotionally devastated, pleading for Lloyd's assistance. Garrison arranged for James's discharge from the United States Navy and took him in as he struggled fruitlessly against the ravages of alcoholism and terminal cancer. As James's health ebbed, Lloyd and Helen nursed him lovingly, encouraging him to put his guilt to rest and to reconcile himself to God by facing his past as forthrightly as possible. When James died in 1842, he left behind a searingly frank memoir that Lloyd had encouraged him to write detailing a lifetime brutalized by alcoholism, exploitation, and abusive living. By playing the role of his brother's compassionate but demanding confessor, Garrison again assumed the role of father, the caring adult presence from which he had never benefitted as a child.

While sharing his brother's fear and pain, Garrison also began to grow increasingly preoccupied with his own physical ailments, perhaps seeing in the dying James an incarnation of his own mortality. Soon his litany of complaints, real and imagined, had grown to include gastric distress, heart palpitations, urinary difficulties, shooting pains, backaches, recurrent headaches, and a mysterious "swelling" of the chest. By age forty, in 1845, Garrison had become a chronic hypochondriac, consulting often with doctors and experimenting ceaselessly with homeopathic medicines, hydropathy, and animal magnetism, nostrums and regimens that led him in turn to an interest in dietary reform, hydropathic medicine, and spiritualism. Nothing pleased him more than conflicting diagnoses, which encouraged still further investigation and discussion of his ailments. He complained endlessly to his fellow clique members, and they always responded with concern and advice, even while joking among themselves about his quirks. In this manner, Garrison satisfied his continuous need for attention and reassurance while confirming yet again that his private life, thanks to his beloved clique, was affording him solace in some of his deeper fears.

As Garrison's personal life grew richer, some aspects of his public role also began to change. From his earliest years a driving preoccupation with self had always shaped the essentials of Garrison's character and fed his zeal for reform. Emerging alone from an emotionally devastating childhood, Garrison's solitary struggle to establish himself had led him to become a preeminently public man. His private estimate of his own self-worth depended on confirming, time and again, his sense of his exalted stature in the public eye. His deepest personal hatreds of passion and disorder could only be addressed by constantly challenging the public with new and more stringent standards of civic morality. Garrison had always measured the purity of his soul by the scorn heaped upon him by a corrupted nation and by his inspired discovery of ever higher levels of truth. Now, however, as the clique and his own personal household merged into one supportive family, Garrison's ideological focus became permanently fixed. Though hating slavery as deeply as ever and as committed as always to immediatism, disunionism, feminism, and perfectionist nonresistance, Garrison nevertheless contributed no further ideological innovations to the ongoing crusade for black emancipation. His zeal for public controversy remained as strong as ever, but igniting it now more often than not were issues that would solidify, not divide, his small but extended abolitionist family and preserve its creeds from revision or challenges.

Throughout the 1840s and 1850s, "Father Garrison" was far more concerned with maintaining his beloved fellowship than in embracing controversial new converts or convictions that might risk discord or division. When, for example, a few of his close colleagues ventured beyond immediatism to link perfectionism with the growing problem of industrial poverty, Garrison's conservative inclinations soon came clear. John A. Collins returned from England horrified by the brutal squalor of industrial Liverpool and was convinced that New England's headlong transformation into a factory-based manufacturing economy was already leading to the same dire results of chronic poverty, a widening gap between rich and poor, an angry working class, and the gradual corruption of all society. While Collins became a disciple of the British utopian socialist Robert Owen and set up a collective farm, Adin Ballou, another perfectionist abolitionist, sought to cure society of the evils of competition by organizing his Hopedale community around spiritualism, temperance, "water-cures," and vegetarian agriculture. Even Garrison's brother-in-law, George Benson, felt compelled to move beyond "the emancipation of the slave to the emancipation of all labor" by selling his farm and launching the North-ampton Association based on profit sharing, cooperative management, and the education of the young in perfectionist principles. Garrison, however, made it clear from the outset that he saw no validity in such experiments. As the industrial revolution spread across New England, creating drab factory towns, increasingly concentrated wealth, and an even larger, more hard-pressed working class, Garrison still firmly rejected all suggestions that labor relations under capitalism partook of enslavement. He certainly agreed that poverty created evils "too dreadful to be contemplated by the human heart." He, too, had blanched at London and Liverpool's slums and had heard the protests of England's working poor. Nevertheless, he also concluded that critics of the capitalist labor market had now set out a challenge to the tenants of abolitionism that he held sacred above all others and that had always inspired him to pursue his self-made career. Moreover, a free society depended most of all on the God-given sanctity of every person's right to exercise his economic, social, and spiritual individuality. The social equality envisioned by Collins, Ballou, and others proposed to stifle those rights, Garrison charged, thereby erecting new forms of enslavement no different from those exercised by the planters of the South. The goals of the utopian socialists were laudable, he granted, but their dreams of suppressing competition between free individuals would actually create not the perfect society, but its antithesis by depriving God's creatures of the right to secure their own destinies. Obliterating industrial poverty, Garrison argued, required a "moral revolution, starting with the individual and working outward." "Individual personal effort," he insisted, "is the true foundation of all prosperity in the social state. No form of society can be devised which will release the individual from personal responsibility. . . It would be the greatest curse that could be inflicted on him." In this most crucial sense, all poor people except those enslaved by a human master always had within their reach the divine opportunity to transcend their degradation: "They may go in rags, it is true, but their bodies and souls belong to them, not others." For this reason, poverty itself could actually be regarded as a blessing, Garrison observed, confronting individuals with the wholesome challenge of transforming themselves into self-made individuals by exercising "piety, self-denial, perseverance and education."

When declaring that poverty must never be confused with slavery, Garrison wore his own scars of deprivation proudly, his family's victimization by a shoe industry that had reduced his mother to a scrub woman's life and him to beggary. Recalling his harsh beginnings from the opulence of Maria Weston Chapman's Beacon Hill drawing room, Garrison had abundant reasons for believing that God's will operated in the marketplace to reward self-discipline and that adversity offered the promise of liberation. Years before, in the very first issue of the *Liberator*, he had not only prophesied his own success ("I WILL BE HEARD"), but had also defended free-labor capitalism as a system "where avenues of wealth, distinction and supremacy are open to all," and his statement still read well after the passage of twenty years. Lionized by the Chapmans, Phillips, Westons, Jacksons, and Quincys, the self-made former apprentice from Newburyport felt no inclination to equate the poverty spawned by factory capitalism with the tyranny of slaveholding, or to fear for the future of the nation's industrial laborers. For Garrison, supporting the forces that were reshaping America into a powerful industrial state went hand in hand with abolishing slavery.

By his own estimate, Garrison and his disunionist circle faithfully lived out among themselves the same ideals of self-liberation that they sought for the nation at large. Although the most patrician among them confirmed in private their feelings of superiority, the blue bloods of the Boston clique usually worked with no hints of antagonism with their colleagues of more humble circumstances. Ready financial assistance, free legal counsel, and other forms of material support from the wealthy in exchange for significant personal favors from the less well-off eased feelings of class resentment. Instead, the same devotion to individualist values that inspired Garrison's denials of class enslavement received endless confirmation in day-to-day activities and personal exchanges that emphasized spontaneity and wide-ranging personal choice. Hence, when one of the clique's freest spirits, Nathaniel P. Rodgers, did dare to suggest that the wealthy immediatists were lording it over their poor associates, that all forms of labor partook of enslavement and that abolitionists, as Christians, must therefore renounce private property, take vows of poverty, and dismantle their governing bodies, Garrison charged treason. Stifling his strong personal affection for Rodgers, "Father Garrison" stepped forward to reassert interclass solidarity within his "family" by having the renegade purged. Assisting him were two aristocrats, Quincy and Phillips, and two militants with humble roots in the New Hampshire backcountry, Parker Pillsbury and Stephen S. Foster. Thereafter, no Garrisonian seriously challenged the powerful ideals of individualism that inspired their crusade and ordered their private world.

Regarding the rights of women, Elizabeth Cady Stanton once claimed that the Garrisonian-dominated American Anti-Slavery Society "is the only organization on God's footstool where the humanity of women is recognized, and these are the only men who have ever echoed back her cries for justice and equality." While generally muting distinctions of class, Garrison's "family" also lived out its commitment to individualism by suppressing almost completely invidious distinctions between women and men. Garrison, as noted, deferred instinctively to powerful women and from the beginning had exalted their power to enrich the enterprise of reform. After his perfectionist Christianity had led him to embrace female political equality as well, women's votes in particular had enabled him to overcome the "new organization" and remain in control of the American Anti-Slavery Society. The imperative of gender equality was thus firmly embedded in the culture of the Boston clique. In his private correspondence and in public remarks Garrison made it clear how much he valued the "wise counsel," "good sense" and "devoted labors" of Maria Weston Chapman and her sisters, a clear extension of the admiration he had once expressed for the Grimkés. To Lucretia Mott, who led the Philadelphia branch of the Boston clique, Garrison gave continuous acknowledgment for spiritual instruction in the Quaker ways of simplicity and humility, and for her "pioneering strength" as one of the earliest immediatist leaders. The strong willed Abby Kelley Foster often disagreed with Garrison, but did so assured that he was a supportive colleague, willing to explore differences candidly and cooperatively. From the haughtiest of blue bloods, Quincy, to the most plebian of perfectionists like Henry C. Wright, Garrison's male associates behaved in most cases with an equivalent respect for women, regarding their contributions as enriching to both the cause and to the redeeming fellowship of the clique itself.

Not surprisingly, women quickly claimed positions of power and responsibility within Garrisonian circles after 1840. When the schism of that year created the need for a new official newspaper for the American Anti-Slavery Society, Garrison was the first to support the appointment of Lydia Maria Child as editor of the *National Anti-Slavery Standard.* She held the post for nearly four years. Male members of the Boston clique also expressed little but satisfaction with the forceful presence on the Massachusetts Anti-Slavery Society Executive Committee led by Maria Weston Chapman, or with Lucretia Mott and Sarah Pugh's contributions on the Board of the American Anti-Slavery Society. When Abby Kelley Foster took up duties as a paid lecturer for that Society, the terms and conditions matched exactly those of her male counterparts. There were, to be sure, special duties calling for domestic skills that fell largely to Garrisonian women, most specifically the organizing of bazaars, fairs, and other such fundraising occasions. But even these responsibilities often involved interested men (Garrison was often one of them) and required entrepreneurial activity that enhanced female self-worth and a sense of collective achievement. Abby Kelley Foster once observed that abolitionist women had powerful reasons to be grateful to the slaves "for the benefit we have received for *our-*

selves in working for *them*. In striving to strike his irons off," she believed, she and her co-workers had also discovered how to begin freeing themselves. Coming from one so critical and committed as Foster, such remarks measured well the Garrisonians' unusual success in overcoming the "sinful coercion" that they saw in "distinctions of sex." By the middle 1840s, Garrisonian abolitionists and the American feminist movement had all but fused into a single crusade, and female abolitionists were contributing a distinctive and compelling moral critique to the war against slavery.

When it came to race relations, however, Garrison's "family" achieved no such happy synthesis. As we have seen, most white abolitionists had always found it difficult to develop a positive view of African Americans and the culture they embodied. Garrison, like nearly all of his white colleagues, had assumed from the first that his Christian duty compelled him to aid the "benighted negroes" in rising from a culture of "ignorance" and "barbarism" to a "civilized" state of middle-class respectability. Despite his condescending viewpoint, African American activists had nevertheless rallied almost as one behind Garrison during the 1830s, heartened by his attacks on colonizationism, his demand for immediate emancipation, and his stringent insistence on obliterating "colorphobia." When he was threatened with mobbings, Boston's African Americans had volunteered as body guards. But during the schism of the late 1830s however, African American solidarity with white Garrisonians had begun to unravel over the issues of women's rights, voting, and religious perfectionism, leaving a growing mutual suspicion and waning mutual support. It became apparent to black Garrisonians, for example, that their white colleagues did not welcome them into positions of power or responsibility. Within the Boston clique itself no African Americans were ever included, although the local African American community contained noteworthy leaders that were highly educated, well traveled, and loyal to Garrison. With the exception of William Still, who served for fourteen years as General Clerk of the Pennsylvania

Anti-Slavery Society, Samuel Snowden, who served on the board of the New England Anti-Slavery Society, and Frederick Douglass, who briefly presided over that same body, African Americans were kept on the margins of Garrisonian management. William Nell, for instance, worked as Garrison's assistant in the *Liberator* office for nearly two decades, but when a higher position was created for which he was qualified, the job went instead to an outside hire who was white.

Ideological disaffection also compounded some African Americans' alienation from white Garrisonians. Many blacks grew suspicious, for example, that nonresistance, women's rights, and perfectionism were extraneous to their deepest interests, and they resented being told by whites not to vote when racist legislation already denied them the ballot in so many parts of the North. But most of all, powerful African American leaders such as Henry Highland Garnet, Frederick Douglass, and Martin Delaney came to resent the ethnocentrism and paternalism that they sensed in their white colleagues' efforts to "civilize" them. To Garnet, such racist arrogance amounted to no less than "a desire to sink me again to the condition of a *slave* by forcing me to think as you do." On the other side of the growing racial rift, some of Garrison's powerful white associates, particularly Maria Weston Chapman and Edmund Quincy, mixed blue-blood snobbery with racist condescension, while others, particularly Wendell Phillips, insulted equally all opponents of Garrisonianism regardless of their complexions. And Garrison, for his part, made it clear to one and all just how zealously he yearned to be the savior of the "wretched colored race." At the same time, white Garrisonians did take great pride in their African American colleagues, giving particular notice to lecturers they employed such as Frederick Douglass and Charles Lennox Remond. In so doing, however, it was usually because such individuals seemed to confirm how "civilized" African Americans could become when properly "cultivated" through their contact with whites. As Lydia Maria Child once observed of Remond, "He is the first colored person I have met who seemed to be altogether such a one as I would have him." Treated too often as the children of the Garrisonian family, some blacks began an exodus in the 1840s, showing a growing desire to rely on organizations that they themselves could control.

One who so decided in 1847 was Frederick Douglass, the most impressive and accomplished of Garrison's African American co-workers. Garrison had met the gifted Douglass in 1841, and the former slave soon began to rival Wendell Phillips as the Garrisonians' most compelling public speaker. After establishing his reputation on the podium and publishing a popular *Narrative* of his life in bondage, Douglass completed a successful tour of Great Britain in 1845 and 1846, accompanied by Garrison. The two traveled together again in 1847, lecturing in Ohio, Pennsylvania, and upstate New York. As his income and reputation compounded, Douglass decided to publish a newspaper of his own, a plan that triggered resentment within the clique and challenged the paternalism of "Father" Garrison. There were already too many abolitionist newspapers, Garrison and others suggested, and Douglass's natural talents made him fit to be an orator, not a thinker and writer. Without consulting further, Douglass moved to Rochester, New York, in 1847, established his *North Star*, and secured the editorial services of Julia Griffith, who was single and white, thereby provoking Garrison's deepest feelings of resentful paternalism and prejudice.

In *Liberator* editorials Garrison condemned Douglass for showing ingratitude toward his white sponsors. Contradicting his long-held position that he had no objections to "race mixing," Garrison charged that Douglass's professional relationship with an unmarried white woman would damage the immediatist cause by raising specious allegations of "amalgamation." Douglass had diminised his moral fitness to "speak for the negro race," Garrison charged, claiming also that Douglass's decision to publish his own paper proved that "there is a roguery somewhere." The *Liberator* refused to reprint selections from the *North Star*, and Garrison even suggested that Douglass's behavior confirmed that the abolitionist movement had become too sophisticated for African Americans "*as a class* to keep pace with it . . . or to understand the philosophy of its operations." Douglass, disgusted, finally renounced his allegiance to disunionism, joined the Liberty party, and condemned his former colleagues for trying to keep him and all of his race in "the short frocks of childhood." "They all talk down there," he complained of the Garrisonians, "as if all anti-slavery ideas originated with them, and that no man has a right to 'peep or mutter' on the subject who does not hold letters of patent from them." Garrison, for his part, would refuse for years to speak to Douglass, whom he privately vilified as "thoroughly base and selfish . . . destitute of every principle of honor, ungrateful to the last degree, and malevolent in spirit." It was an embarrassing display of prejudice, showing Garrison's abolitionism in its narrowest and most bigoted aspects.

In light of such incidents it is noteworthy that so many African Americans remained fervent supporters of Garrison, and that even Douglass continued with the American Anti-Slavery Society for nearly three years after the onset of this controversy. Independent-minded activists such as William Nell, John T. Hilton, Charles Lennox Remond, Robert Purvis, Charlotte Forten, and William Whipper knew well that white Garrisonians, for all their faults, could always be counted as relentless foes of segregation and other forms of public discrimination. Garrison and his friends possessed resources, organizing skills, and a burning desire to overthrow segregation, which proved crucial whenever African Americans took up the battle against discrimination. Garrison's unremitting hatred of coercive restrictions on an individual's God-given freedom applied no less to segregation in Boston than to bondage in the South.

In July 1841 the militant David Ruggles gave Garrisonians the chance to put their convictions into practice. Refusing to sit in the "blacks only" section of a steamship bound for Nantucket, he was expelled by the captain, only to return the next month to invade a car reserved for whites of the New Bedford Railway. After receiving a manhandling, he took the railway to court.

When the judge held in favor of the railroad, Garrison denounced the decree as "unspeakably atrocious," and most of the clique packed off immediately to New Bedford. There, Garrison volunteered to organize a protest that would overturn the discrimination through an irresistible application of militant nonresistance. On August 10, Garrison, Phillips, Douglass, Parker Pillsbury, John A. Collins, and about forty other abolitionists of both races simply overran the segregated steamship from which Ruggles had been ejected, by sheer numbers forcing the helpless captain to capitulate. Crowding on to the "negro deck" the integrated group held an impromptu antislavery meeting, complete with resolutions condemning segregation and pledging to overturn it.

In the course of that meeting Garrison opposed on the usual nonresistance grounds a motion by Stephen S. Foster to require all abolitionists to engage in such public confrontations, but happily endorsed as an individual the instigation of boycotts, nonviolent "ride-ins" and litigations across Massachusetts against the New Bedford and the Boston-Portsmouth and Eastern Railroads. Each week thereafter in the *Liberator* Garrison published a full column of railroad schedules, accompanied by denunciation of those that made "vile complexioned distinctions, enforced by brutal assaults." He traveled frequently together with his African American *Liberator* assistant, William Nell, and always in the "blacks only" car, a practice he continued whenever necessary for the rest of his life. Following the clique's direction, the *National Anti-Slavery Standard* officially endorsed the boycott on behalf of the American Anti-Slavery Society, and Ellis Gray Loring and Wendell Phillips testified against the railway companies before the Massachusetts state legislature.

Finally, fearing a legislative defeat, the railroad companies capitulated voluntarily, and Garrisonians of both races honestly congratulated one another for having achieved a notable collaborative victory. Garrison's moralistic penchant for denunciation and public displays of his own rectitude had harmonized nicely with the African Americans' goal of mitigating a system of day-to-day oppression and humiliation, and the white Garrisonian "family" had proved themselves reliable co-workers with Douglass, Ruggles, and the rest. Whatever their races, moreover, all these abolitionists firmly believed that the boycotts, lawsuits, and acts of civil disobedience were integral to pursuing their elusive goal of moral revolution, for widespread public appeals transcended local issues and challenged the whole North to face its deep-rooted complacency and racism. Some Boston African Americans in 1846 went so far as to exclaim to Garrison that "even the stages and steamboats are now open to us by your instrumentality." The fairer estimate, though, was that Garrison and his white friends had made a strong and uncompromised supporting contribution in the African American struggle for self-liberation.

The most impressive instance of Garrisonian collaboration with African American activism involved the desegregation of Boston's public schools, an arduous eleven-year struggle that blacks led and in which members of the clique played crucial roles. The same William Nell whom Garrison failed to promote stood at the center of this conflict, distinguishing himself as a leader with few peers. In 1829, Boston's mayor had refused to include Nell, though fully deserving, in a city-sponsored banquet recognizing outstanding graduating seniors. By 1846 Nell was repaying this never-forgotten insult, joining with another prominent local African American, John T. Hilton, to campaign for the desegregation of the city's public schools. When an extensive petition campaign to the Boston School Committee failed, boycotts and tax protests began, spurred by the revelation that a white principal of an all-black school was a chronic absentee who also punished his students cruelly. Next came massive public demonstrations, threats of violence, and an expensive litigation that led, unsuccessfully, to the Massachusetts Supreme Court. Following this judicial defeat, boycotting continued until 1855 when the state government finally outlawed all distinctions of color and religion in Massachusetts's schools. The victory, above all, gave eloquent testimony to the tenacity, skill, and vision of Nell, Hilton, and the hundreds of black Bostonians who supported them.

Yet throughout this arduous campaign, the whites of the Boston clique also exercised a profound impact on the direction of race relations in their city. Since Boston had no African American newspaper, the *Liberator* continuously served that function, publishing notices of meetings, news of legislative events, reports of the proceedings of the Boston School Committee, and a stream of supportive editorials by Garrison. Nell and Hilton also enjoyed full access to the *Liberator*'s columns, publishing articles over their own signatures, soliciting donations, and furnishing their supporters with essential information. Garrison also joined Phillips, May, Quincy, and the Weston sisters (who ran their own integrated private academy) at protest meetings where he rose more than once to rain denunciation on Boston segregationists. Phillips nearly exhausted his rich vituperative talents in a series of editorial attacks on both the School Committee and on Horace Mann, the hard-pressed State Commissioner of Education. When the state antisegregation law finally passed in 1855, Hilton, Nell, and the others arranged a celebration dinner at which Garrison and Phillips were invited to be the only white speakers. Addressing the gathering, Garrison praised William Nell and proclaimed that the victory clearly confirmed the unstoppable power of the self-liberated individual. This great triumph, like all moral revolutions, Garrison maintained

> begins in the heart of the solitary individual, humble men and humble women, unknown in the community, without means, without power, without station, but perceiving the thing that ought to be done, loving the right in all things, and having faith in the triumph of what is just and true, engage in the work, and by and by, the little leaven leavens the whole lump, and in this way the world is to be redeemed.

"It is impossible to do right," he concluded, and "be defeated."

As Garrison's statement makes all too clear, his romantic individualism left him quite unmindful of the enormous collective black effort that actually had created this victory. Remond was far more accurate when praising his co-workers' "self-sacrifice," "consistency," and willingness to undergo "endless drudgery." Nevertheless, there could be no question that when their local community had faced a crisis caused by intolerable racial injustices, Garrison and his white "family" had served the African Americans well. Though never meeting the egalitarian expectations of their black associates, Garrison and his circle set a standard for social involvement that few white Americans dared to emulate, then or since.

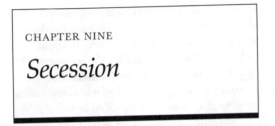

CHAPTER NINE

Secession

Though as suspicious as ever of partisan politics, Garrison recognized that slavery questions bore heavily on the 1844 presidential election. Since the late 1830s, antislavery feeling among northern voters had been stimulated by the mob violence against abolitionists, the petition campaigns and the gag rule struggle in Congress, by several spectacular slave mutinies on the high seas, and by a growing Yankee reluctance to enforce the constitutionally mandated Fugitive Slave Law of 1793. In this setting, it was hardly surprising that northerners in large numbers bridled at the renewed prospect of adding another slave state, Texas, to what seemed an already menacing "slave power." Nevertheless this was what the Democratic party nominee, James K. Polk, proposed, even though Texas annexation promised war with Mexico, which still refused to recognize the independence of its former province. Such a conflict, in turn, could yield still more lands for slavery—the vast expanses of California, Arizona, New Mexico, Nevada, and Utah.

To satisfy northerners in his party, Polk also promised annexation of the Oregon territory, a large area ill-suited for slavery that was jointly occupied by the United States and Great Britain. The Whig nominee, Henry Clay (whom Garrison dismissed as a "mountebank"), found no equivalent strategy for uniting North and South. Since some of his most vociferous northern allies rejected Texas annexation on antislavery grounds and most of his Southern supporters felt strongly otherwise, Clay tried to avoid the issue. Meanwhile, the Liberty party that

Garrison so hated drew strength from these sectional tensions. Party members renominated Birney, demanded legislative emancipation, opposed Texas annexation, and condemned slave owners for corrupting the two-party system. It was clear to Garrison that the noise of electioneering was drowning out his lonely cry for "No Union with Slaveholders," at least for now. "Just at the moment," he confided, "we are reserving our anti-slavery strength and preparing to make an onslaught on public sentiment as to the disunion question as soon as the Presidential campaign shall have terminated." By 1846, however, Polk had claimed the White House, Texas had been annexed, and hostilities with Mexico were underway. Garrison now had compelling new reasons for launching his "onslaught on public sentiment."

In Massachusetts, politics quickly divided over slavery. By 1845 newcomers such as Charles Sumner, Charles Francis Adams, and Henry Wilson were moving to the forefront of a "conscience" Whig insurgency, demanding an end to the party's tolerance of slavery's further expansion. In New Hampshire the rebellious Democrat John P. Hale challenged his party to arrest the spread of slavery, while in New York and Pennsylvania more dissident Democrats also came forward. In Ohio, antislavery Whigs led by Joshua Giddings explored coalition with the Liberty party and established close ties with Sumner and his Massachusetts colleagues. As American troops marched through Mexico, the nation's governing system began a slow evolution toward sectional crisis, and righteous Garrison, in electoral self-exile, worked to hasten the political reckoning.

As Garrison was well aware, his stark disunionism developed compelling political currency as conflicts grew over the "free soil" issue. Even before 1844, in fact, free-state politicians had begun to echo Garrison's disunionist warning that slavery was taking an ominously corrupting hold on American values and institutions. In 1843, for instance, twelve northern congressmen led by John Quincy Adams had declared that Texas's annexation would subvert the Union's legal basis, and two years later, the state legislatures in both Massachusetts and Ohio passed similar resolutions. Giddings, in Ohio, made opposition to the Mexican War the basis of a disunionist platform for his 1846 re-election to Congress. In their own ways, all these political figures were articulating feelings familiar to Garrison which carried them well beyond conventional legalism and party loyalty, even though, unlike Garrison, their versions of disunionism really demanded northern supremacy within the 1787 compact by preventing the further expansion of slavery. Nevertheless, they, like the Garrisonians, had become deeply repelled by political allegiances that tied them so closely to the planter class. In this important respect, Garrison's disunionism and the fears of the free-soil politicians began to coalesce as the sectional crisis intensified. For in a fundamental sense, Garrison's diagnosis of the Constitution was proving all too true, and politicians were increasingly willing to state that the Union protected the slave system. "Men who would have whispered disunion with white lips a year ago now love to talk about it," observed an enthusiastic Wendell Phillips. "Many leading men will talk as we were laughed at for talking a while ago."

But Garrison also knew that professional politicians like Giddings, Hale, or Adams rejected all thoughts of actually renouncing the Constitution, ending their careers, and turning away from electoral combat against the "slave power." Though their rhetorical appeals against the Union did confirm the power of Garrison's constitutional critique, they nevertheless sought to arrest slavery through legislation. For this reason, Garrison warned them constantly, insurgent free soilers were repeating the Liberty party's "fatal mistake" of "giving fealty to this bloody parchment." Worse still, none of them ever publicly embraced the doctrine of immediatism, and many made clear their conviction that "free soil" meant preserving the western territories for white free laborers alone, revealing an inherent antipathy toward African Americans whether enslaved or free.

Garrison, however, had been fascinated since his youth by the same political process that he denounced as corrupt, and in a way he even envied these insurgent politicians who hated slavery but spurned the moral revolution. In a rapidly expanding free market of antislavery ideology, their "flawed" doctrines now were far outselling his own, casting still further doubts on the substance of his claim of leadership and vision. Eager to reconfirm his political pertinence no less than his prophetic status, Garrison began proclaiming in the mid-1840s that the movement to stop the spread of slavery arose as the natural consequence of the abolitionists' morally superior demand to dissolve the Union. The sudden appearance of political insurgents like Sumner, Giddings, Hale, and the others, he argued, simply reflected the rapidly transforming moral vision of grass-roots voters who were being revolutionized by Garrisonian agitators. And since "politics will always be shaped by its morals," Garrisonians needed only to continue their disunionist cries in order to magnify their political influence. Their accumulating power, Garrison prophesied, would be measured as the political crisis over slavery expanded, driven forward by revolutionized voters who sloughed off their corrupt loyalties and elected leaders opposed to the slave power. "The nation must be abolitionized before our abolition Congress can be created," he insisted. Garrison now had begun to sense, however vaguely, the nature of his final vindication. Should the political conflict someday shatter the Union and emancipation result, the victory would be his and his fellow disunionists' for inspiring such a moral revolution.

To be sure, Garrison's theories were rife with contradictions. How, critics wondered, could he claim as his creations the very politicians whose constitutionalism he denounced? For his part, moreover, Garrison could never stifle the vain hope that all politicians and voters would suddenly rush to his disunionist banner. But for a censorious prophet anxious to retain his purity while shaping the future to fit his will, his theories were endlessly self-reinforcing. His insightful critic, Nathaniel P. Rodgers, once charged that Garrison and his friends were "purblind with politics," for while refusing to vote they "loved to kick up political dust" by hovering "around the polls to watch the

balloting of others, and about the statehouse where they can enjoy the turmoil of legislature." In exactly this fashion, Garrison
now chafed to involve himself in the politics of the free-soil
movement.

His most promising opportunity lay in Boston with the "conscience" Whigs. By 1845, Sumner, Wilson, Charles Francis Adams, and John G. Palfrey were openly defying the Whig party's
"cotton" leadership, and in response Phillips, Quincy, and
other clique members quickly involved themselves on their own
disunionist terms, endorsing no candidates but kicking up political dust whenever they could. Garrison harried the "cotton"
Whigs in the *Liberator*, assisted by Quincy, who was by far the
Garrisonians' most trenchant political writer, and Phillips
joined Garrison at anti-Texas rallies in several parts of the state.
At one of these gatherings, in December 1845, Garrison served
as an elected delegate and was "rapturously applauded" after
delivering his disunionist opinions and congratulating the "conscience" Whigs for their patriotism and courage. Afterward,
Garrison helped maintain the conflict's momentum by quarrelling over Texas with the Boston *Advertiser*, the "cotton" Whigs'
leading newspaper, while encouraging Sumner and the rest to
"snap the cords of party and stand up untrammelled in the
cause of the slave." Garrisonians, he explained, were "anxious"
to give every "conscience" Whig "a full measure of credit for
what he has done, and to sustain him as far as he is disposed to
go in his opposition to the Slave Power." Proving the value of his
political word, Garrison vociferously supported "conscience"
Whig John G. Palfrey when Palfrey defied his party as a United
States Congressman in 1847 by refusing to support "cotton"
Whig Robert C. Winthrop as Speaker of the House. While Phillips sent Palfrey private congratulations and attacked Winthrop
viciously in several speeches, Garrison in the *Liberator* scorned
the enraged protests of "cotton" Whig editors and kept the controversy before the public.

Meantime, of course, he attacked vociferously the selfsame
politicians he was claiming as his creations and castigated all

who continued to cast ballots. Every individual "must be cured of the madness of politics or their damnation is sure," he declared, and "must be drawn from the polls as they are from the grogshop or the house of ill fame, by the conviction of sin." Anxious to confirm that he remained uncorrupted by his own engagement with politics and that he was still heard in his self-styled prophetic role, he assailed most furiously the leaders who scorned and ignored him. But when free-soil politicians such as Giddings, Hale, and Sumner seemed to listen respectfully to his criticisms, Garrison was also quick to praise their "unfailing good temper" and "nobility of soul" in holding themselves "amenable to censure." Instead of being "abusive or malignant," he observed, these politicians "understood the intentions of...Phillips and Quincy and Pillsbury and Foster too well to fly into a passion," and he judged it a pity that all politicians could not "heed such an example or profit from it." Antislavery politicians, in short, had become for Garrison still another audience, and a crucial one at that. How they responded to his disunionism had now become in his mind a continuing measure of his public stature and of the political pertinence of moral suasion. For their parts, some antislavery politicians, particularly Giddings, Henry Wilson, and Sumner, cultivated close friendships with individual Garrisonians and seemed to value the debates over disunion. Others such as William Seward and Charles Francis Adams had no time whatever for such "fanaticism."

Satisfied that disunionism was inspiring the politics of free soil, Garrison boarded a schooner for England in July 1846, just as the Mexican War began. If the political requirements of moral suasion required him to defy the Constitution, its underlying religious imperatives compelled him to continue unmasking the corruption of proslavery Christianity. Just as had colonizationists and new organizationists years before, malignant proslavery forces within the United States were again threatening the integrity of worldwide abolitionism, Garrison feared. He had discovered, for instance, that slaveholding Presbyterians had sent substantial cash donations to the Free Church of Scotland, clear evidence to him of a conspiracy by corrupted church-goers to stifle reform within the English-speaking Christian community. In a closely related development, Protestant clerics on both sides of the Atlantic had joined to create an evangelical alliance designed to unite English-speaking Protestants against "popery" and religious heresies like his own perfectionist anti-clericalism. Even though his closest advisors, Phillips and Quincy, felt these issues did not justify the expense of such a voyage, Garrison got his way.

Charles L. Remond, James Buffum, and Henry C. Wright had agreed to join Garrison in England, where his oldest English friend from the 1830s, George Thompson, also awaited him. Frederick Douglass also joined Garrison's party, having fled to Britain to avoid the possibility of reenslavement, once his popular *Narrative* had revealed his identity and location. Stopping first in London, Garrison's entourage participated briefly in the World Temperance Conference, where a competing delegation led by the hated Lyman Beecher treated them with open contempt. Far more heartening was the meeting he attended several days later, with Thompson serving as chair, that created Great Britain's first formally organized Garrisonian antislavery society, the Anti-Slavery League. Before his tour had ended, additional outposts of the League had been established by his supporters in Dublin, Ireland and Glasgow, Scotland. Their avowed purpose was the global destruction of slavery through the power of moral suasion. The League condemned the United States Constitution, the Liberty party, the "new organization," the Free Church of Scotland, and the Evangelical Alliance. To Garrison, it almost seemed like the glories of the 1830s were returning once more: "It was a real, old-organization antislavery meeting," he reported excitedly to Helen, "such as was never before held in this metropolis. . . . I made a long speech which elicited the strongest marks of approbation, and was received by the assembly with a tempest of applause, they rising from their seats, swinging their hats and cheering loudly."

Accompanied by Douglass, Thompson, and Wright, Garrison next invaded the Evangelical Alliance's organizational meeting, interjecting provocative questions that threw the proceedings into satisfying disarray. Then, for three months, Garrison and Douglass toured the British Isles, demanding that the Free Church of Scotland "send back the money," denouncing proslavery Christianity, and urging "No Union with Slaveholders." In his "eighteen years of anti-slavery experience," he declared in tones that invoked the wisdom of an earlier age, he had seen "nothing more wicked or malicious, more wanton and cruel," than the influence "emanating from the apologists of the Free Church and the Evangelical Alliance." Judged against the explosive controversies that were driving the nation to sectional crisis, these wars against obscure religious enemies meant almost nothing. But for Garrison personally, the memories they evoked of his earliest victories sharpened his zeal and renewed his visions of victory and vindication.

Though tinged with nostalgia, Garrison's renewed battles with proslavery religion reflected deep feelings of anticlericalism that now pervaded the entire crusade against slavery. Within the American Anti-Slavery Society, a growing perfectionist drive to "come out," that is, to separate from all coercive and enslaving religion, grew ever more common and disruptive. Beginning in the mid-1840s, two harsh-spoken Yankees, Stephen S. Foster and Parker Pillsbury, explored the furthest boundaries of abolitionist "come-outerism" by nonviolently interrupting church services with discordant condemnations of organized religion. Parishioners' surprise invariably turned to outrage as Pillsbury or Foster would suddenly rise during the sermon to declare loudly: "Your ministers are blind guides and reprobates, your churches, cages of unclean birds." Usually, the offending abolitionist found himself thrown bodily out the door. But while Quincy, Phillips, Chapman, and May, among many others, winced at these tasteless displays, Garrison offered no objection to Foster and Pillsbury's excesses for he, too, was now eager to brand the ministry as "a brotherhood of thieves," the "haughty, corrupt, implacable and pious foes of the anti-slavery movement." "Steeped in blood and pollution as the American Church is," read one Garrison-sponsored resolution, "it becomes us to turn from it in loathing and abhorrence." By 1848, Garrison's deepening alienation from organized religion had led him to organize an abortive campaign for an "Anti-Sabbath Convention" and to announce to his *Liberator* readers that he no longer believed in the revealed truths of Scripture. "The Bible," he declared, was "a self-evident falsehood," an erroneous compilation of lies and superstition, fabricated over the centuries by corrupted clergymen. Only by exposing this "tyranny of scripture," Garrison charged, could the truly pious hope to live by the "simple example of our non-resistant Savior."

For all its hyperbole, Garrison's anticlerical fulmination, like his disunionism, spoke cogently to some of the nation's deeper anxieties. By the middle of the 1840s, many opponents of slavery, not just perfectionist Garrisonians, had begun to feel repelled by the clergy's decades-long refusal to speak forthrightly against the "peculiar institution" and by the hollowness of sacramental worship. Some, like Lewis Tappan, withdrew to found "free churches," independent of any denomination, in which slavery was held sinful. Others continued to battle within the denominations, causing deep dissention and severe losses of membership among Baptists and Congregationalists. Within the Methodist church, formal division took place in 1845, leaving hostile pro- and antislavery wings. Other pious opponents of slavery left their national denominations to form "purified" sects such as the Free Presbyterian Church, the Progressive Friends, and the Franckean Lutherans. Meanwhile, many lifelong abolitionist leaders undertook private spiritual odysseys away from organized religion. Theodore Weld, Angelina Grimké Weld, Gerrit Smith, Elizur Wright, Jr., William Jay, and Lydia Maria Child, for example, all rejected denominationalism entirely for spontaneous personal experiences, scrapping formal theology and faith in Scriptures for a diffuse "religion of humanity." By striving to become (as one such seeker put it) "less orthodox but more Christian," such abolitionists quietly parallelled the boisterous anticlericalism of Foster, Pillsbury, Garrison, and Henry C. Wright while seeking to disentangle themselves from all relationships that could corrupt one's quest for harmony with Divine Law. As loyalty to established creeds and institutional churches continued to erode, Garrison was joined by many who were initiating their own spiritual civil wars.

Garrison returned from Great Britain in November 1846 to a political situation that seemed well along in fulfilling his prophesies of moral confrontation. As American forces claimed vast sections of Mexico and the presidential election neared, the free-soil disruption of northern politics continued to spread. Hoping to diffuse sectional tensions, the Whigs and Democrats selected war heroes to head their tickets and adopted platforms designed to remove the slavery extension issue from the campaign. Whig Zachary Taylor avoided the question while Democrat Lewis Cass stood for popular sovereignty, which left to the citizens of any new state the decision of whether or not to admit slavery. Voters in antislavery districts now clamored for political revolt. In 1848 most of the Liberty party merged with dissident Whigs and Democrats, holding a nominating convention in Buffalo to form the Free Soil party. Former President and once-vociferous antiabolitionist Martin Van Buren headed a ticket that demanded free soil and northern supremacy within the Union but that also remained mute on the necessity of slave emancipation. With the hope of somehow securing black liberation through a party largely dedicated to the interests of whites alone, Leavitt, Stanton, Whittier, Bailey, and others now cast their lot with the Free Soilers.

As his hated opponents made these obvious compromises, Garrison, triumphant, claimed their choice was a total confirmation of the wisdom of disunionism. The Free Soil Party, he righteously declared, "is attempting to make brick without straw—to live without food...No Union with Slaveholders!" A few Liberty men such as Gerrit Smith and William Goodell spurned the "tainted" Free Soilers for a fourth party based on legislated emancipation and they, too, received only Garrison's contempt. But when Free Soilers launched a series of rallies in Massachusetts, Garrison was enthusiastically in attendance, observing the "brutish workings" of the party he had just condemned and claiming it as the product of his labors. The political system seemed to be moving towards crisis, and he relished the prophetic role he now claimed for himself and his fellow disunionists. While Edmund Quincy wrote editorials in the *Liberator* warmly encouraging the Free Soilers on disunionist grounds, Garrison hailed the party "as a cheering sign of the times, and as unmistakable proof of the progress we have made in changing public sentiment." Unlike the retrograde Liberty party leaders, he now insisted, Free Soilers had rebelled "for conscience sake" against the shackles of an enslaving two-party system and deserved "commendation and sympathy" from the same Garrisonians who challenged them with the "higher position" of "No Union with Slaveholders."

When the ballots were tallied, it seemed to many besides Garrison that prophesies of sectional rupture might indeed prove true. While Zachary Taylor captured the Presidency, the Free Soil party made a surprisingly strong showing, electing a dozen United States Congressmen who commanded the balance of power in the House of Representatives. California petitioned for immediate admission to the Union while militant Southern politicians threatened secession unless slavery were granted open access to all lands obtained as a result of the war with Mexico. Slaveholding Texas, now a state, also threatened secession unless the federal government agreed to expand its boundaries and absorb debts Texas had contracted during its years as an independent republic. For over a year, in 1849 and 1850, the nation's government was gripped by unprecedented sectional deadlock. While the *Liberator* urged contending politicians to embrace the solution of peaceful disunion, Garrison began sensing that the moment of moral revolution might truly be at hand. "I long to see the day," he revealed to Helen, "when the great issue with the slave power of the dissolution of the Union will be made by all the free states, for the conflict will be a short and decisive one. The Free Soil movement inevitably leads to it," he assured her, "and hence I hail it as the beginning of the end." Time, of course, would prove Garrison's prophesies tragically false. When the South, not the North, declared for secession, the conflict that followed was hardly to be short and decisive. But whatever the accuracy of his predictions, Garrison, though still a fervent pacifist, had now begun to think in terms of force, rather than nonresistance, as the probable final impetus to emancipation.

As it turned out, American political leaders achieved compromise, not confrontation, for the time being. Led by Stephen A. Douglas, Henry Clay, and Daniel Webster, Congress finally passed a battery of legislation designed to restore harmony between the sections by eradicating all contention over slavery. California was admitted as a free state, the federal government absorbed Texas's debts, and in the remaining territory conquered from Mexico slavery extension questions were left for resolution by popular sovereignty. To placate the North, slave trading, but not slavery, was abolished in the District of Columbia, while to compensate the South, Congress greatly strengthened the Fugitive Slave Law of 1793. Federal commissioners, not state judges, were to decide fugitive cases, and any northerner who assisted escapees risked severe penalties. Those accused as fugitive slaves were deprived of jury trials, the protection of writs, and the opportunity to testify, exposing even legally free African Americans to the threat of seizure and enslavement. As Congress approved this legislation, Garrison's excited prediction of "the beginning of the end" appeared hopelessly erroneous. So did his inflated claim that disunionist agitation was inspiring a political reckoning with slavery. Instead, it seemed by the end of 1850 that slave emancipation had once again become as remote a possibility as it had been twenty years earlier, when Garrison had first set forth on his crusade.

It might indeed have seemed to Garrison that the 1850s were recreating his earliest memories of the struggle against slavery. Just as the Jacksonians had done in the 1830s, patriotic crowds quickly gathered in every northern city to celebrate the preservation of the Union and to voice their contempt at all who questioned it. Massachusetts's premier Whig statesman, Daniel Webster, captured the mood perfectly in Faneuil Hall, dismissing the abolitionists as "rub-a-dub" fanatics who deserved to be scorned as the nonentities they really were. As politicians everywhere celebrated the Union, antagonistic mobs also began to reappear, as Garrison and his colleagues discovered in New York City when attending the annual meeting of the American Anti-Slavery Society. Egged on by James Gordon Bennett, vituperative Democratic editor of the New York *Herald*, mobs of Irish Catholic workers turned the abolitionists' meeting into chaos for two full days before Garrison finally admitted defeat and called the police. Later that year, a second unruly gathering further renewed Garrison's memories of the turbulent 1830s. George Thompson returned to Boston, and Garrison tried to arrange a welcome for his friend in Faneuil Hall. Instead, Webster's supporters turned out in force and disrupted the meeting completely, leaving only when the police arrived and ordered everyone home. And in politics, antislavery all but expired when the Free Soil party's leading figures became involved in state-level coalitions with the Whigs or Democrats. During the presidential election of 1852, the Democrats pledged undying support for the compromise measures and easily carried the nation for New Hampshire's Franklin Pierce.

Contemplating these circumstances, abolitionist veterans of every persuasion felt a mounting sense of frustration and discouragement. For all of them, Garrison included, the glorious day of slave emancipation now seemed further away than ever. Twenty years of moral suasion had yielded not black liberation but an increase of nearly a million in the total number of slaves. The political geography of slavery had also expanded greatly, magnifying all the more the influence of the planter class in the nation's government, economic development, and cultural life. Some abolitionists grew disillusioned and began moving on to more rewarding endeavors. Elizur Wright, Jr., a mathematical genius, discovered an extraordinary new career in life insurance reform, while Theodore Weld pioneered in early childhood education. James G. Birney, exhausted, sought solitude in the northern Michigan wilderness. Many other veteran abolitionists, however, began venting their frustrations by exploring more direct and militant ways to combat the slave power. As they did so, Garrison's leadership slowly began to diminish.

The new fugitive slave law, a masterpiece of legislative injustice, symbolized perfectly all of the abolitionists' frustrations. From the moment of its enactment white reformers of all persuasions, African American activists, and free-soil militants alike, emphasized their common determination to render it unenforceable. Fugitive slave rescue incidents quickly multiplied all over the North, totalling over eighty by 1860. Boston set a national example of resistance. In 1851, for example, angry citizens of both races forcibly rescued a much-surprised fugitive named Frederick Wilkins by seizing him from the courtroom where his trial was being conducted. Soon after, another such group was unable to liberate Thomas Sims, despite a series of large and threatening protest meetings. May 1854 witnessed the most extraordinary confrontation of all when Boston's militants failed to rescue the fugitive Anthony Burns when an armed mob stormed the courthouse and accidentally killed a guard. President Pierce ordered the city occupied with two thousand federal troops, some of whom were reputed to carry live ammunition.

As these breathtaking events unfolded practically before his doorstep, Garrison remained remarkably uninvolved. He was happy to devote many pages in the *Liberator* to news of every case, editorialize hotly against the Fugitive Slave Act and its supporters, and rejoice in print at every successful rescue. Yet the primary responsibility for pushing the campaign forward quickly fell into other hands. Joining Wendell Phillips (who had always been skeptical of nonresistance) were recently recruited

activists, hot-eyed men who had become involved in abolitionism too recently to have been influenced by the pacifist tradition
of moral suasion. Feeling few compunctions against arming
themselves or others, Thomas Wentworth Higginson, Samuel
Gridley Howe, and George Luther Stearns joined with Phillips,
Theodore Parker, and two former Garrisonians, Henry Bowditch and Ellis Gray Loring, to form Boston's Vigilance Committee. They aimed to render the Fugitive Slave Act
unenforceable in Boston, but did not invite Garrison to join
them. His perfectionist pacifism, they decided, disqualified him
from leadership in their new crusade. "Garrison was thrown
into the background," one Boston militant recalled. "Forcible
resistance to the black law was now obedience to God."

Garrison harbored compelling personal reasons for avoiding
situations such as fugitive rescues that might require him to give
direct support to acts of violence. His Christian pacifism, as discussed, arose in part from a compelling lifelong hatred of uncontrolled passion that always made mobs repulsive to him.
Long before, moreover, he had placed nonresistance at the heart
of his abolitionist theology, making it central not only to his
public mission, but also to the rich friendships he enjoyed with
his fellow saints of the Boston clique. Now however, the abolitionists' heightened desire for confrontation and their increasing willingness to apply coercive measures had begun to weaken
the integrity of "Father" Garrison's extended family, a trend
that drove him still further away from the work of the Vigilance
Committee. Phillips now abandoned the clique for long periods,
organizing local vigilance efforts and preaching armed resistance from platforms across New England. Garrison's dear
friend, Samuel J. May, long a nonresistant, confessed to Garrison that his hatred of the Fugitive Slave Law was forcing him to
renounce his pacifist faith. As some of his closest companions
struck off on their own, newly active militants such as Higginson, Howe, and Stearns seemed to be shouldering him aside to
claim front-rank positions in the intensifying struggle. Garrison
began complaining that these hotheads were too often seeking

"glory" in their own "hostility" and that "on that capital they set up an antislavery reputation." Such upstarts, he insisted, gave "no proof of anti-slavery fidelity" when compared to those who continued their moral "warfare not only against slavehunting alone, but against the existence of slavery" as well.

As the Vigilance Committee plotted strategy without him, Garrison drew inspiration from the extraordinary popularity of Harriet Beecher Stowe's *Uncle Tom's Cabin* published in 1852. The long-suffering figure of Uncle Tom himself reassured Garrison of the enduring power of nonresistance since "no insult, no outrage, no suffering could ruffle the Christ-like meekness of his spirit." Deeds of violence and the enduring love of the Savior still seemed wholly incompatible to him. Still, Garrison could not explain how Uncle Tom and his three million fellow slaves would actually be liberated, unless Tom himself, or someone else, rose up to vanquish his oppressors. Short of civil war or servile insurrection, the problem was one that no other American could resolve either, and in this respect Garrison's hopeless insistence on a peaceful transformation of all the nation's values can seem, in retrospect, disarmingly insightful, as his colleagues in ever-increasing numbers discarded the ethical standards of the moral revolution for the compulsion of violence. Seeking different answers than Garrison's to this perplexing question, Phillips began delivering rhetorical masterpieces that extolled the violent valor of Crispus Attucks, the African American patriot, and Toussaint L'Ouverture, the Haitian insurrectionist. Foster, Pillsbury, and Henry C. Wright continued to claim fidelity to nonresistant principles but adjusted them alarmingly in order to urge slaves to violence. Venturing further still, Higginson, Sterns, Howe, Parker, Gerrit Smith, Frederick Douglass and a few others began to wonder just how an insurrection of slaves might actually be instituted.

While abolitionists searched for a feasible means of confrontation, politicians found it in May 1854, when the Democratic party sponsored the enactment of the Kansas-Nebraska Act. This legislation, demanded by southern Democrats, repealed

earlier legal restrictions against slavery's expansion into Kansas
or Nebraska enacted by the Missouri Compromise of 1820. Slavery's future status would now be decided instead by applying
the principles of popular sovereignty. Stephen A. Douglas, the
legislation's principle sponsor, remarked that he cared little
whether "slavery was voted up or down" in these territories. An
extraordinary number of northern politicians and voters felt
passionately otherwise, however, believing that the Act revealed
a monstrous plot by slaveholders to convert frontier lands once
reserved by law for free white laborers into a despotism inhab-
ited by "tyrannous" master and "degraded slaves." Editors and
orators all over the North joined with Garrison to protest that
this latest assault by the slave power stood "against the laws of
God, the rights of universal man—in subversion of plighted
faith, in utter disregard for the scorn of the world, and for purposes as diabolical as can be conceived here on earth." The
Whig party collapsed and northerners deserted the Democrats
in droves as the pressure of renewed sectionalism finally destroyed the two-party system. By late 1854, northern citizens
from all political backgrounds had come together to endorse
free soil and adopt the name of the Republican party. The elements of Garrison's long-anticipated confrontation over the
nature of the Union had begun to fall into place. Even as the
faithful deserted his banner of nonresistance and youthful militants discounted his leadership, Garrison found himself facing
an antislavery-minded audience of unprecedented size.

By all the standards he believed in so deeply it was, of course,
a "partial, half hearted" audience, "blighted" by an active prejudice toward African Americans, a marked distaste for slave
emancipation, and a narrow constitutionalist commitment to
"free soil." And it soon became clear, too, that this much-
expanded free-soil revival would lead to some truly bloody consequences which were repugnant to his nonresistance creeds.
The Kansas-Nebraska Act touched off a sectional footrace as
free-state and pro-southern immigrants rushed to the territory
and struggled to control the election that was to decide the fu-

ture of slavery. Soon these contests degenerated into guerilla warfare, and abolitionists as diverse as Lydia Maria Child, Gerrit Smith, and Wendell Phillips actually welcomed the news of frontier bloodshed, arguing that the killing of proslavery opponents fulfilled their devotion to freedom's higher laws. By 1855, old line "cotton" Whigs in Boston such as Amos Lawrence had begun collecting funds to arm free soilers in Kansas, drawing the support of Garrison's most violence-prone associates, the newcomers Higginson, Howe, and Stearns as well as the ever more vehement Phillips and Parker.

Though increasingly isolated in his devotion to nonresistance, Garrison found himself attracted to this vast political upheaval as well as repelled by it. The unchecked westward march of slavery, the bloody reports from Kansas, and the collapse of the two great parties all gave compelling credence to his prophecy that slaveholding provoked the deadly judgments of a righteous God. The emerging Republican party, moreover, reconfirmed in his own mind his claims for the political effectiveness of disunionist agitation in rousing the voters against slavery. Yet there could also be no question that powerful free soil politicians and apostles of abolitionist coercion, not Garrison, were dictating the course of the revivified struggle against slavery. As colleagues rejected his doctrines of nonresistance and as a massive political movement engulfed his own, Garrison's deepest worry returned to trouble him once again. In this cacophony of ever-multiplying and hostile voices, who was listening to him? Nearly twenty-five years before, he had found the promise of his life's fulfillment when vowing to everyone, "I WILL BE HEARD!" Now deeply concerned that his prophesy might be proving hollow, he traveled to Framingham, Massachusetts to preside at the Fourth of July celebration of the Massachusetts Anti-Slavery Society. As the abolitionists gathered, Anthony Burns had just been returned to slavery and Congress had just given approval to the Kansas-Nebraska Act.

The meeting in Framingham was the most self-advertising occasion that Garrison ever arranged. As abolitionists convened for the out-of-doors celebration, the platform set up in front of them was draped in black crepe. Behind the rostrum hung an insignia of Virginia (Anthony Burns's dire destination) festooned with ribbons of triumph. Next to it and "hung with the crepe of servitude" was the seal of the Commonwealth of Massachusetts. Above the rostrum flew two flags, bearing the names of "Kansas" and "Nebraska." And suspended in the background of the entire tableau was the American flag, bordered in black and positioned upside down. Few remembered what Garrison said at this gathering, but far more important was the nation's shocked reaction to the ritual he performed. Fearing that he was losing his audience, Garrison needed to give graphic confirmation that he and his cause could still command headlines and stun the conscience of the nation.

Concluding his remarks with a reading from Scripture, Garrison closed his Bible, lit a candle, and told his listeners that he would now perform a ceremony that bore witness to his deepest beliefs. Picking up a copy of the Fugitive Slave Act he held it to the flame, named it, raised it aloft and challenged his audience as it burned: "And let the people say 'Amen'!" "Amen," they responded, with sober conviction. Next, he burned the two legal findings that had returned Anthony Burns to slavery. Again the incantation and the response—"Amen." Finally, he raised a copy of the United States Constitution, pronouncing it "a covenant with death, an agreement with hell." It blazed brightly as he held it aloft and declared, "So perish all compromises with tyranny!" The audience's "Amen!" echoed across the Massachusetts countryside.

Garrison was again attempting to reclaim the past in order to force the future to conform to his deepest wishes. And again, the future proved impervious to his influence. Back in 1831, his initial promise never to "equivocate" or to "give one inch" had been fired by a fresh and compelling vision that had called forth an inspired host of young crusaders behind the banner of immediate emancipation. Burning the Constitution, by contrast, was simple theatrics that could never infuse new life into Garrison's shopworn doctrines or flagging capacity to inspire. But the gesture, as he hoped, did gain him national attention and refreshed his reputation for censorious extremism. It also contributed heavily to the angry atmosphere of sectionalism and spoke compellingly to the abolitionists' mounting frustration. It could not, however, save his dwindling crusade for moral revolution from free soil politicians and platform warriors.

Unable to reclaim his mantle of leadership, Garrison began slowly and quite unconsciously to accommodate to the mounting tempo of violence. Though protesting in all sincerity his unflagging devotion to nonresistance, he also began to applaud deeds of violence, committed by others, that he refused as a pacifist to condone for himself. News of armed resistance by Kansas free soilers in 1856 prompted him to praise these guerrillas' "great forbearance" before returning force with force, and to declare that "from a patriotic standpoint they deserve to be ranked with the men of 1776." He believed, for himself, that "the duty of returning good for evil at all costs" and "the inviolability of all life . . . should rule over all human affairs," those in Kansas included. But given the corruption of a sinful and violent world, armed resistance by free soilers was now, for Garrison, far preferable to unchallenged slaveholding tyranny on the great plains. In his own estimation, Garrison still remained as uncompromised as ever by a world where politics and violence now mingled in ever more equal proportions. But at the same time, he freely gave his benediction to those who faced the slave power with guns in hand. "There is not a drop of blood in my veins, both as an abolitionist and as a peace man," he admitted in 1856, "that does not flow with the northern tide of sentiment" to defeat the "barbaric and tyrannical slave power."

As Garrison's bastions of nonresistance crumbled, he turned increasingly to the Republican party to confirm the meaning of his twenty-five year crusade. That party, to be sure, deserved the same scorn he had bestowed on the Liberty party and the Free Soilers, and Garrison was quick to condemn roundly its "feeble," "indefinite," "partial," and "one-sided" nature. But while clinging to northern disunionism and his personal refusal to vote, he plainly encouraged others less sanctified than himself to give their electoral support to the Republican cause. That party, he continued to claim, owed its very existence to the Garrisonians' success in transforming the values of voters in the North. "In general intelligence, virtuous character, humane sentiment, and patriotic feeling," he declared in 1856, "as well as in the objects it seeks to accomplish, it is incomparably better than those other rival parties, and its success *as against those* parties will be a cheering sign of the times." When the Republicans nominated John C. Frémont for President against the Democrats' Buchanan, Garrison went further still, issuing in the *Liberator* what many read as an editorial endorsement: "It seems to us the sympathies and best wishes of every enlightened friend of freedom must be on the side of Frémont," he admitted. If "there were no moral barrier to our voting, and we had a million votes to bestow, we should cast them all for the Republican candidate." After reading this statement, Republican editor Horace Greeley quickly pressed Garrison about his personal intention to vote for Frémont, and Garrison replied, as always, "No Union with Slaveholders!" But despite these avowals he was now exhibiting unmistakable symptoms of wishing that he, too, could join the antislavery parade to the ballot box. As the Republicans gathered their strength, Garrison felt himself increasingly divided by his conflicting desires to preserve his moral purity and to join the party that was, perhaps, the harbinger of his vindication.

In the aftermath of the 1856 campaign, in which the Republicans competed effectively despite Buchanan's victory, Garrison vividly demonstrated how deeply he felt these quarreling impulses. Hoping that Frémont's defeat would heighten Republican interest in actually repealing the United States Constitution, Garrison launched a vain attempt to capture the allegiance of the same politicians whose party he yearned to call his own. In January 1857, he convened a disunionist convention in Worcester, Massachusetts, and invited Republican luminaries such as Henry Wilson, Joshua Giddings, Charles Francis Adams and others to join the proceedings. Garrison envisioned a meeting where elected officials would sit with disunionists like himself and Phillips and actually plan "measures to effect a peaceful withdrawal" of the North from the South. The results of such deliberations, he hoped, would lead to a still larger national disunion convention involving abolitionists and Republicans from all parts of the North in a sweeping collaboration to undo the federal government. Needless to say, Wilson, Adams, Giddings, and the rest shunned this opportunity to plot strategy with the Constitution-burning Garrison and his friends, and the meeting provided simply another occasion for Phillips, Higginson, and Parker to demand disunion and threaten violence. Garrison upheld the standard of pacifism as best he could, but withdrew his support from the national disunionist convention that was to follow. His attempt to secure a position within the Republican party on his own disunionist terms had failed miserably. Instead, he found himself being whipsawed all the more by contrary yearnings for moral revolution and for open war with the slave power.

Garrison was hardly alone as he struggled against his impulses to endorse ballots and bullets. Within the ever-thinning ranks of the "old organization," debates on these matters grew even more intense, and some of his closest friends sorely tested his lingering commitment to nonresistance. At the 1857 annual meeting of the Massachusetts Anti-Slavery Society, Henry C. Wright, zealously claiming pacifism, nevertheless argued vehemently that true abolitionists must furnish arms for slave insurrections. In this debate Wright enjoyed the full support of Phillips, Higginson, and the Fosters, and Garrison, struggling to sustain the high ideals of moral revolution, barely managed to sustain a majority to vote down Wright's resolution. The following year's meeting brought forth even deeper conflicts when Abby Kelley Foster and Steven S. Foster announced that moral suasion and northern disunionism were now bankrupted causes. Impressed by the rapid growth of the Republican party, the Fosters now argued that direct political action, including voting, represented the only effective approach for ending slavery. "Our people believe in a government of force," they emphasized, "but we are asking them to take an essentially non-resistance position which is wholly inadequate.... they wish to vote." Higginson and Parker Pillsbury then seconded the Fosters' resolution to "build a great national party whose aim shall be the overthrow of the government." Garrison was hard pressed to maintain a disunionist majority as he defended his nonresistant creed: "It is *not* my duty to contrive ways for men in union with slavery, and determined to vote without regard to the moral character of their act, to carry out their low ideas," he declared adamantly, "and I shall not do such work." When Foster's motion went down to narrow defeat, Garrison had once more confirmed his political independence and his control over the old organization. Yet his arguments surely rang hollow to all who recalled his near-endorsement of John C. Frémont. The Boston clique had plainly begun to dissolve, and "Father" Garrison, who shared his friends' conflicting yearnings for victory and purity, possessed no resource with which to arrest the process.

John Brown, however, had little patience with these Garrisonian agonizings over the uses of force. Brown and his followers invaded Harper's Ferry, Virginia, in October 1859, hoping to incite slave insurrections. Garrison had no foreknowledge of this daring plan, but when hearing the news of Brown's raid, he was probably not altogether surprised. He and Brown had spent an evening, two years earlier, in Theodore Parker's home disagreeing vehemently about the morality of nonresistance, and of Garrisonianism in general, and Brown was known to have complained, "These men are all talk; what is needed is action— action!" Yet some of abolitionism's most prominent figures such as Higginson, Stearns, Frederick Douglass, and Gerrit Smith helped finance Brown's attempt at insurrection, and others like Wendell Phillips gave money and asked no questions. Directly supported by some abolitionists and condoned by others, Brown's raid fulfilled half-articulated desires for vengeance and victory that had been growing in abolitionism since the Compromise of 1850.

As reports of Brown's capture, trial, and execution galvanized the nation, Garrison, like practically every abolitionist, explained away whatever remained of his nonresistant's creed. At first, Garrison was genuinely repelled by Brown's act of naked terrorism. The raid, he declared, was "misguided and wild, and apparently insane," though "disinterested and well intentioned." But as Brown began to orchestrate his own martyrdom by issuing compelling statements from his jail cell, Garrison's devotion to pacifist ideals could finally hold out no longer. Wholly unwilling to recognize that he was actually abandoning doctrines that had preserved his sense of purity for nearly thirty years, he finally capitulated to the pressures of confrontation by revising his nonresistance doctrines to the point of near meaninglessness. In this way he never had to examine his tenacious belief in the continuity of his personal morality or to admit to the fruitlessness of his demand that the nation transform its fundamental moral structures. In public, however, there could be no question that Garrison had joined Phillips, Higginson, Parker, and many other militants in support of Brown's insurrection.

On the eve of Brown's execution, Garrison addressed a crowded protest meeting in Boston's spacious Tremont Temple and made his new position clear to everyone but himself. After reading from Brown's final statement to the public, Garrison asked nonresistants in the audience to identify themselves. When only a solitary voice replied, Garrison publicly compromised his pacifist principles while insisting to all within earshot that he was still just as uncompromised a nonresistant as ever. Willing now to endorse violent deeds by others that he refused to undertake himself, he invoked, "AS A PEACE MAN":

> Success to every slave insurrection in the South and in every slave country. And I do not see how I compromise or stain my peace principles in making that declaration. Wherever there is contest between the oppressed and the oppressor . . . God knows that my heart must

be with the oppressed. . . . I thank God when men who believe in the right and duty of wielding carnal weapons are so advanced that they will take those weapons out of the scale of despotism and throw them into the scale of freedom. It is an indication of progress and positive moral growth; it is one way to get up to the sublime platform of non-resistance; it is God's method of dealing retribution on the head of the tyrant.

Though he was incapable of acknowledging it, Garrison had now clearly descended from his lofty, prophetic position to mix directly in the nation's political crisis. Compromised in his espousals of nonresistance, there was now far less to distinguish him from thousands of others who rallied to the tune of "John Brown's Body" and prepared to vote Republican in the 1860 elections. To be sure, Garrison still demanded two uncompromised measures that Republican politicians scorned—immediate emancipation and northern disunion. Moreover, he still refused to vote. Yet his ringing endorsement of Brown's insurrection had undermined the pacifism that had for so long allowed him to preserve his claim of transcendent independence. His acceptance of the Republican party on its terms, not his, was only a matter of time.

The moment came in the midst of the 1860 presidential campaign which matched Abraham Lincoln against the divided Democrats' Stephen A. Douglas and John C. Breckinridge and the candidates of several minor parties. Following the election carefully, Garrison, as always, withheld his ballot, called for northern disunion, and castigated the Republicans as a "time-serving, temporizing and cowardly party." Yet these were the habits of ritual, acquired over two decades. What was truly new about this election, Garrison claimed, was the fundamental transformation he now observed in northern politics, a change that betokened the imminent arrival of his much-prophesied moral revolution. "The pending election," he declared, "witnesses a marked division between the political forces of the North and South" that touched on issues far more fundamental than slavery's expansion. It "really signifies," he wrote, "a much deeper sentiment in the breasts of the people of the North, which in the process of time must ripen into more decisive action." What this "more decisive action" would actually be, Garrison failed to predict. Nevertheless, it was clear from his statement that he now looked to Republican voters, not disunionist saints, to act as the vanguard of the struggle with slavery. By comparison, his near-endorsement of Frémont four years earlier seemed a model of equivocation.

While revealing that his hope for moral revolution now rested with the Republican party, Garrison, for once, showed acute political judgement. Since the passage of the Kansas-Nebraska Act, northerners in ever-increasing number had come to believe that a vast "slave power conspiracy" now moved, unchecked, against all of America's liberties. Following Frémont's loss to Democrat James Buchanan, the United States Supreme Court had announced its decision in the case of *Scott* v. *Sandford*, issuing sweeping pronouncements that gave slaveholding interests unquestioned theoretical supremacy under the United States Constitution. To the widespread dismay of people in the North, the Court had decreed that Congress had no power to legislate limits to slavery's expansion, that African Americans were to have no legal rights that whites were "bound to respect," and that slavery, in essence, was to really enjoy all the explicit constitutional protections pointed out so scathingly by Garrison in the first place. The Dred Scott decision had truly ignited that "much deeper sentiment in the breasts of people" which Garrison now welcomed so warmly. How many more demands would they be forced to satisfy, northern voters wondered, before this southern juggernaut commanded the nation's destiny? What was to become of their vision of America as an expanding free-labor civilization, ever renewing itself as independent, God-fearing farmers and artisans moved westward, to create a bountiful countryside where liberty flourished? Demanding unequivocally that slavery's dominion be ended forever, Republican voters declared their intention to meet the South in direct political battle.

In earlier times the Republican's demand for "Free Soil, Free Labor, Free Men" would hardly have satisfied Garrison's stringent standards of moral revolution. But as he accustomed himself increasingly to the dictates of power politics, he judged the news of Lincoln's election as a nearly acceptable equivalent. "Babylon has fallen!" he exclaimed at the news of Lincoln's victory, and he rejoiced in his firm identification with "our grand, magnificent, invincible North." "Give me the omnipotence of the North," Garrison exclaimed in early 1861, "give me the resources of eighteen free states...on the side of freedom, as a great independent empire, and I will ask nothing more for the abolition of slavery." Lincoln's victory had solidified northern political power, and citizen Garrison, though still preaching disunion, now demanded that this power be wielded unsparingly. His years of calling for a peaceful revolution of American political values had finally ended.

With Lincoln's inauguration, secessionists organized in earnest throughout the deep South. Garrison, in turn, took his final leave of perfectionism by rushing to the defense of the now imperiled Union. In the minds of many planters, the Republican party was a direct instrument for abolition for several compelling reasons. No matter how emphatically Lincoln rejected legislated emancipation or the idea of race equality, it was clear that he and many other powerful Republicans regarded slavery as a perversion that must not expand and ought, eventually, to be eliminated. With Lincoln in power, planters feared, abolitionists like Garrison would be given free run of the South, stirring up insurrections and inflaming jealousy among poor, slaveless whites. Also denied the expansion so necessary to their survival and facing subversion from without and within, slaveholders felt secession was the only possible escape. They seized the chance by firing on the federal arsenal of Fort Sumter in South Carolina. Lincoln called for 75,000 volunteers to put down the rebellion and refused to compromise. As soldiers drilled on Boston Common, Garrison and almost all of his disunionist colleagues elected at once to march under the flag of Union victory.

For Garrison, the journey to patriotic militarism was quick and simple, accomplished through the now-familiar process of self-deception that always allowed him to preserve his sense of moral purity. First, he denied that his demand for northern disunion had ever accorded an equivalent right of succession to the South. Had the North seceded in peace, he explained, its motives would have accorded with the highest dictates of God's will. Southern secession, by contrast, was simply an act of proslavery treason, "the concentration of all diabolism" that must be crushed by northern armies. Preventing secession with military might, Garrison now argued, was simply a logical extension of his righteous demand for "No Union with Slaveholders." With his moral consistency again reaffirmed, Garrison went on to declare that the "total, wonderful and indescribable" revolution he saw in northern public opinion signalled the fulfillment of his disunionist crusade. The "morals of the people" were now being "wholly transformed," he declared, creating a government that Christians must protect by force of arms since it now possessed the power to legislate and enforce immediate emancipation.

This, for Garrison, was truly the crux of the matter. As the slave states left the Union and the North mobilized for war, he saw clearly in the crisis of the Union the vindication which he had pursued for a lifetime. Since his vow in 1831 to be "HEARD," he had warned an uncaring nation without ceasing that "the one great cause of all our nation's troubles and division is SLAVERY," and that its "removal" was "essential to our national existence." Now that the abolitionists' "predictions have come to pass," he demanded, "are they to indulge in morbid exclamations against the natural law of inevitable justice, and to see in it no evidence of...the power of truth, or the approach of the long-wished-for jubilee?" As cannons rolled and troops began to march, Garrison happily declared that the way had been "opened for a glorious redemption." Slavery would soon be given the "death blow, . . . complexional prejudices shall swiftly disappear, injurious distinctions cease and peace and good will everywhere reign." With the vision of emancipation to guide him, Garrison was finally marching toward Zion, and towards the day of Jubilee when his lifelong quest for fulfillment and recognition would finally end in triumph. On that day, shackles would fall from these million slaves while Garrison, secure as ever in his independence and purity, shared fully in their moment of emancipation.

CHAPTER TEN

Fulfillment

As warfare commenced in earnest by December 1861, Garrison removed the motto "NO UNION WITH SLAVEHOLDERS" from the *Liberator*'s masthead and replaced it with a passage from Isaiah: "PROCLAIM LIBERTY THROUGHOUT THE LAND, TO ALL THE INHABITANTS OF THE LAND." With the covenant with death now annulled forever, abolitionists everywhere, Garrison foremost among them, began pressing Abraham Lincoln to wield his power as supreme commander to emancipate the slaves. They all believed Lincoln needed to be pressured unrelentingly, particularly because his prewar record on slavery issues gave them little reason for optimism. During the 1850s Lincoln had advocated colonization, had upheld the 1793 Fugitive Slave Law, and had even represented a master in court seeking the return of an escapee, earning him Wendell Phillips's famous sobriquet "Slavehound from Illinois." In 1861, moreover, the *New York Tribune*, like other Republican Party newspapers that spoke for the administration, made it clear that maintaining the Union, not abolishing slavery, should be the overriding goal of the war: "The war is, in truth, a war for the preservation of the Union, not for the destruction of Slavery and it would alienate many ardent Unionists to pervert it into a war against slavery."

Sharing their deep concern over Republican timidity, Garrison eagerly joined Phillips, Douglass, Gerrit Smith, and other abolitionist luminaries in condemning Lincoln's cautious approach and restricted vision. "It is more and more evident that he is a man of small calibre; and had better not be at the head of a government like ours, especially in such a crisis," Garrison complained privately in late 1861. When, for example, Lincoln countermanded the battlefield orders of two generals who would have freed slaves in occupied parts of the Confederacy, Garrison sided with his appalled colleagues in charging the President with "a serious dereliction in duty" that proved him "a dwarf in mind." As Lincoln further persisted in valuing the loyalties of the border states and conservative Republicans above the advice of the abolitionists, Garrison led his co-workers in circulating emancipationist petitions which exhorted immediatists to protest to Congress, and addressed Lincoln bitingly in the *Liberator*: "To refuse to deliver these captive millions in tantamount to the crime of their original enslavement and their blood shall a righteous God require at your hands." And in early 1862 when Lincoln attempted to revive a program of colonization, Garrison again vented his frustration: "Lincoln may colonize himself if he chooses," he stated, "but it is an impertinent act, on his part, to propose getting rid of those who are as good as himself."

To his followers this was the familiar Garrison, suspicious of "time serving" politicians, rejecting secular power as corrupting, and anxious to defy conventional wisdom. Yet for all his attempts to maintain fidelity to lifelong abolitionist principles, there was no denying that Garrison had already made many concessions to the world of power politics, beginning with his near-endorsement of John C. Frémont in the 1856 presidential election. By 1861 he had, in actuality, all but stationed himself in the Republican camp by encouraging voters to elect Lincoln and by scrapping nonresistance for the sake of Union victory. The Republican party, whatever its flaws, did seem to offer the promise of final defeat for slavery, the ultimate fulfillment of Garrison's personal crusade, and as the realities of an ever-widening and still more brutal war began to reveal themselves, Garrison's support for Lincoln and his party grew even stronger and more obvious. Backing Lincoln whenever possible seemed now to offer the only way to reach the goal of emancipation, the only result that could justify so murderous a conflict and insure for the abolitionists their ultimate victory. By 1862, as Union defeats and casualties multiplied, Garrison had completed his evolution from insurgent critic to Republican party loyalist.

Though Garrison did remain skeptical about Lincoln's day-to-day judgments, it was soon clear to all his colleagues that he now intended to ally the American Anti-Slavery Society as closely as possible to the President and to the Republican party. Indeed, he insisted privately that public censure of the administration by abolitionists must be moderated, or even cease altogether, in total contradiction to his decades of political criticism. "I have always believed," he wrote in complete seriousness to Oliver Johnson at the *National Anti-Slavery Standard*, "that the anti-slavery cause has aroused against it a great deal of uncalled-for hostility in consequence of extravagance of speech and want of fact and good judgement on the part of some most desirous to promote its advancement." In other words, it was now time for abolitionists to abandon their traditional calling as agitators. "It is no time," he counselled Johnson, "for minute criticisms of Lincoln. All our sympathies must be with the Government." When Phillips, Franklin Sanborn, Samuel Gridley Howe, Moncure Conway, and other prominent Bostonians formed a militant Emancipation League designed to pressure the Republicans toward more radical policies, Garrison declined to participate.

Instead, as Garrison was quickly discovering, his patriotic defenses of the Republicans and the Union were gaining him widespread popularity and public respect. Courting notoriety as an intransigent critic no longer interested him, for it certainly was far more satisfying to receive recognition from his fellow citizens as a prophet deserving of honor. Regarding himself increasingly as a venerated statesman rather than a contentious agitator, Garrison traveled to New York City to deliver a major address in January 1862. Officials of the Cooper Union had invited him there to speak on "The Abolitionists in Relation to the War," and his reception was not disappointing. Eager to praise his "heroism" on that occasion as one who had "stood

fearless and faithful amid universal defection for thirty years"
was young Henry Beecher, son of Garrison's oldest evangelical
nemesis Lyman Beecher and a compelling spiritual voice for a
rising generation of Yankee Protestants. And personally escort-
ing him to the platform was another representative of the nation's emerging leadership, Theodore Tilden, managing editor
of the powerful New York *Independent* and a consistent supporter
of Lincoln's policies.

Garrison glowed with pride as he heard this influential younger man introduce him as an "unqualified hero" whose "unflinching perseverance" and "unblemished reputation for
truthfulness" made him a "peerless example for all the ages."
Then, as if to give confirmation of the public's approbation of
his career, a woman came forward from the audience to place
flowers and a victory wreath next to the podium just as Garrison
was ascending to the rostrum. The audience burst into loud applause. It was little wonder that Garrison's ensuing remarks
identified Abraham Lincoln's successes with his own and proclaimed the war as fulfilling the abolitionists' crusade. "I am
now with the Government," he emphasized, "to enable it to
constitutionally stop the further ravages of death, and to extin-
guish the flames of hell forever." It was likewise predictable that
he responded to his audience's expressions of adulation by proclaiming his continuing fidelity to his oldest and deepest convictions. In 1862, no less than in 1832, he declared proudly, "I am
an original, uncompromising, irrepressible, out-and-out, unmistakable Garrisonian abolitionist." As the Cooper Union
again shook with applause, Garrison must have envisioned a
perfect reconciliation between his original vow never to compromise and his newfound role as the defender of the Republican
party. Henry Ward Beecher thought it "a great day that we have
lived to see, when Mr. Garrison is petted...and praised by
Governors and judges and expectants of political preferment."
"What," he asked, "is the world coming to?" Garrison's answer
was that at long last the world had recognized him as the
prophet who had always spoken truly of slavery. While he was

hardly the only abolitionist to achieve popular esteem, Garrison was certainly among the first to equate public recognition with this final vindication.

Unlike Garrison, however, his old ally Wendell Phillips believed that the appreciative notices meant only that abolitionists were in danger of selling their principles too cheaply, especially if their popularity led them to support a "weak-willed" President who refused to abolish slavery forthwith. By 1862, the articulate Phillips had moved to the forefront of an emerging group of antislavery dissenters in and outside of Congress who grew increasingly restive both with Lincoln's cautious approaches to emancipation and with the Republican majority's emphasis on preserving the Union. In Congress, several senators such as Ohio's Benjamin Wade and Michigan's Zachariah Chandler now spoke strongly against Lincoln, as did Henry Wilson and Charles Sumner. In the House, George W. Julian of Indiana, Henry Winter Davis of Maryland, Thaddeus Stevens of Pennsylvania, and George Boutwell of Massachusetts also began demanding the abolition of slavery, not simply as a military necessity, but as a moral imperative. As Phillips aligned himself with this growing circle of political insurgents, he also attracted the support of such abolitionist veterans as the Fosters, Charles L. Remond, Frederick Douglass, Gerrit Smith, and Elizabeth Cady Stanton, who were equally critical of Lincoln's refusal to emancipate. Glimpsing in civil war the possibility of social revolution, Phillips and his circle now had little patience for Garrison's change of focus. Indeed, their insistence that slavery could never be *truly* abolished until all the nation's civil codes had been revised to insure racial justice denied explicitly Garrison's contention that the abolitionists' crusade was near to achieving its highest goals.

From the beginning of their close association, important differences between Garrison and Phillips had been subsumed by their common hatred of slavery. Phillips, the Harvard-bred attorney, had always retained an abiding belief in the powers of law and government to liberate individuals, equalize races, and promote economic democracy. As a ceaseless student of history and staunch Calvinist, Phillips had never agreed with Garrison's religious perfectionism or nonresistance. Instead, Phillips held to the view that societies were always being reshaped by monumental struggles between tyrannous aristocrats and enlightened patriots who, like himself, inspired the populace to expand the boundaries of their own freedom. Phillips's abolitionist vision, so unlike Garrison's, ultimately fixed on the power of the state, mandated by popular will. In this mind, equality between the races required the enforcement of powerful legal codes, as yet unwritten, that would magnify the powers of the poor and the excluded. While Garrison had always regarded himself as a speaker of religious truths, Phillips had drawn imperatives from a mythology of Anglo-Saxon republicanism, linking his crusade in his own mind to the struggles of Sam Adams, Thomas Paine, Edmund Burke, and Oliver Cromwell, who had inspired the people to forcefully reshape their governments in the service of liberty. Garrison, the perfectionist visionary, discerned in the war the promise of spiritual deliverance. Phillips, the republican radical, sensed the possibility of social revolution. Their conflicting attitudes towards Lincoln's leadership naturally resulted from these deeper disagreements.

By early 1862, to Garrison's open dismay, Phillips, Foster, and Pillsbury were denouncing Lincoln unsparingly in speeches and editorials while interjecting strongly anti-Lincoln resolutions at antislavery society meetings. In response, Garrison began offering counterresolutions declaring the government "wholly in the right" and defending Lincoln's conduct of the war as giving "high grounds for encouragement." At the April 1862 meeting of the Massachusetts Anti-Slavery Society, Phillips presented motions censuring Lincoln as "culpable" for perpetuating slavery. Garrison and his supporters only narrowly defeated them. Though victorious in this instance, Garrison's control over organized abolitionism was clearly slipping as immediatists divided over his claims of impending victory and Phillips's contrary condemnations of Lincoln.

As the old community of saints continued to dissolve, Phillips traveled to Washington, D.C., to pressure politicians with demands for total emancipation. Some of Garrison's foremost supporters began concluding that the time had now arrived to set the cause aside. In September 1862 Lincoln had proclaimed a partial emancipation policy to take place starting on January 1, 1863, which would free slaves only in areas of the Confederacy not occupied by Union troops. While Phillips rejected the measure as a "sham" and even Garrison criticized its "circumlocution and delay," Maria Weston Chapman, the Weston sisters, and J. Miller McKim all resigned from the American Anti-Slavery Society, declaring a complete victory over slavery and calling instead for philanthropic efforts to "uplift" the emancipated slaves. Garrison criticized these resignations as premature, but also observed that "we are very near the jubilee" and made clear his belief that once Congress had legally abolished slavery, further agitation by abolitionists would be superfluous.

Hence, when January 1, 1863, brought the actual implementation of Lincoln's Emancipation Proclamation, it surprised no one that Garrison's last reservations about Lincoln's leadership vanished, and with them any remaining doubts about the imminent glorious ending of the abolitionist cause. News that the Emancipation Proclamation had become official reached him in Boston while he was attending a Beethoven concert in the Music Hall. The Fifth Symphony was interrupted while the audience gave nine cheers for Lincoln and three for Garrison and the abolitionists. The next day's *Liberator* announced Garrison's conviction that Lincoln now needed only to "finish what he has so largely performed" by enforcing the Proclamation to the letter of the law through an emancipation amendment to the United States Constitution. "Glory Hallelujah!" he declared to an exuberant meeting of the Massachusetts Anti-Slavery Society. "Thirty years ago, it was midnight with the Anti-Slavery cause; now it is the bright noon of day, with the sun shining in its meridian splendor." For Garrison, as for Samuel J. May, the

Westons, Oliver Johnson, Edmund Quincy, and many other clique members, their thirty-year battle was all but over.

For Phillips, Foster, Pillsbury, and Frederick Douglass, however, the struggle for African American equality seemed finally to have commenced in earnest. To Phillips and his supporters, as to radical Republicans in Congress, true emancipation required much more than a presidential proclamation or even a constitutional amendment outlawing slavery. Citing the section in the American Anti-Slavery Society's *Declaration of Sentiments* that had pledged abolitionists to seek complete racial equality, Phillips, Foster, Douglass, and others now demanded a revolution in American black-white relations that would guarantee economic self-determination for emancipated slaves while securing for them the fullest exercise of their citizenship. To this end, Phillips insisted, rebel estates must be confiscated and distributed to liberated slaves, leading Confederates must be disenfranchised, and their former bondsmen guaranteed full access to the vote. All African Americans, moreover, must also be accorded complete civil equality before the law, enforced whenever necessary by the power of occupying Union armies. In other words, the end of the war required all true abolitionists to redeem their original commitment to racial equality by obtaining for the freed people access to land, to education, and above all, to political power through the ballot. Anything less, as Phillips emphasized time and again, would simply guarantee "a South victorious," for embittered planters would reassert their dominance and "leave the negro in a condition little better than slavery." From the perspective of such militants as Phillips and his supporters, Garrison's cries of "Hallelujah" made no sense whatsoever and represented a grave threat to the vital interests of the former slaves.

The question of Abraham Lincoln's reelection in 1864 soon brought these profound disagreements into full public view. Phillips could be found assailing Lincoln's plans for reconstructing the South before distinguished audiences of Republicans and calling for the President's replacement at the head of the ticket in the 1864 election. Garrison, for his part, made clear at self-congratulatory abolitionist gatherings his eagerness to see the antislavery societies dissolved and Lincoln reelected. On one such occasion, Frederick Douglass objected to Garrison's statements by declaring that abolitionists must never disband until "the black man in the South and the black man of the North shall have been admitted fully and completely into the body politic of America." In so arguing, Douglass was clearly registering the opinions of the absent Phillips as well as his own, and by 1864, Phillips's and Douglass's alienation from Lincoln had led both to join an insurgent attempt to prevent the President's renomination. They preferred General John C. Frémont who, they felt, had proven his abolitionist credentials by attempting to emancipate slaves with battlefield directives, and who seemed committed to a thoroughgoing reconstruction of the secessionist states. While Phillips and other disaffected Republicans attempted to convince Frémont to contest Lincoln's renomination, Garrison flew to Lincoln's defense. Though he worried some about Lincoln's "excessive lenience" in approaching reconstruction, Garrison professed no patience for any attempt to undermine the "Great Emancipator."

The annual meeting of the Massachusetts Anti-Slavery Society in January 1864 witnessed the first face-to-face debate on the issues between Garrison and Phillips, and Garrison emerged the clear loser. Phillips delivered blunt warnings about the South's intransigence, branded Lincoln as a bigot who "does not recognize the negro as a man," and called for southern land redistribution, black male suffrage, compulsory education of freed people, and a constitutional amendment barring racial discrimination. He concluded with a resolution opposing Lincoln's reelection as President. Garrison then leapt to his feet, offered a substitute motion which endorsed Lincoln's reelection and disagreed vehemently with Phillips's assessment. "I do not believe a word if it," Garrison exclaimed. "In my judgement, the re-election of Lincoln would be the safest, wisest course." When the vote was finally taken, Phillips's resolutions prevailed by a three-to-two margin. The Massachusetts Anti-Slavery Society was now committed to opposing Lincoln's second term, was on record as favoring social revolution in the South, and was controlled by a majority loyal to Wendell Phillips.

The defeat itself meant far less for Garrison than the dynamics that lay behind it. A significant number of abolitionists clearly rejected the conviction of abolitionist victory that Garrison now embraced as confirmation of his impending vindication. But by the defending Lincoln so ardently, Garrison also seemed to Phillips and others to be opposing all efforts to create a truly republican South and a nation whose laws secured freedom and justice to people of both races. Garrison and Phillips confronted each other once again at the May 1864 meeting of the American Anti-Slavery Society, where their fundamental clash of assumptions became even clearer. When Phillips charged Lincoln with opposing black suffrage, Garrison correctly insisted that extending the franchise to emancipated slaves was not necessarily consistent with the abolitionists' cause, calling it a new issue not addressed in the American Anti-Slavery Society's founding *Declaration of Sentiments*. He would not, he insisted, endorse an immediate granting of the franchise since voting was an earned privilege of citizenship, not an inherent human right. This time, Garrison's pro-Lincoln resolution prevailed over Phillips's impassioned demand for an endorsement of black, male suffrage. What had begun in 1862 as a dispute between Garrison and Phillips over Lincoln's approach to emancipation had now evolved into more fundamental disagreement over the meaning of racial equality itself.

In 1864, Lincoln began developing a reconstruction policy for conquered portions of Louisiana, and his approaches to the status of the freed people came immediately into question. Earlier in the war, troops commanded by radical Republican General Benjamin Butler had occupied New Orleans. Once in control, he had fashioned a regime that repressed disloyal whites and protected the civil rights and economic interests of emancipated slaves. Lincoln, however, replaced Butler as military governor in

1864 with Nathaniel Banks, an old "cotton" Whig. Under the state's antebellum constitution, Banks conducted elections that returned many of the old planter class to power and created a labor system that forced former bond servants to work under very restrictive contracts and furnished them no political rights. Phillips immediately attacked this change of policy as clear evidence of Lincoln's hostility to racial equality and his willingness to sponsor the return of slavery in disguise. Garrison, in the *Liberator*, made clear his opposing opinion that Lincoln's intervention in Louisiana was instead a necessity, because Banks's policies were designed to remedy Butler's social chaos through the gradual "uplift" of the culturally backward freed people. Banks, according to Garrison, was proving himself "the friend, the benefactor and the liberator of the colored people of emancipated Louisiana," while to Phillips "Banks freedom" meant simply "no freedom, none whatsoever." In their differing estimates of Banks's and Lincoln's policies, the irreconcilable perspectives of the Christian paternalist and the political revolutionary stood fully revealed.

When endorsing the Banks regime, Garrison believed sincerely that he remained consistent with principles that had guided him from the outset of his career. At the beginning of the war he had made clear his belief that the slaves' emancipation meant simply "the recognition and protection of his manhood by law—the power to make contracts and receive wages, to accumulate property, to acquire knowledge, to dwell where he chooses, to defend his wife, children and friends." Now that the onset of reconstruction brought Garrison face-to-face with the problem of securing those goals, he resorted to the same missionary impulse to improve the black race that had always shaped his thinking during the antebellum decades. Freed people required not the right of immediate citizenship, he argued, but "preparation for assuming such rights," especially through programs that would educate them, reinforce their Christian piety, and teach them the values of sobriety, thrift, and regular labor. "When was it ever known that liberation from bondage was accompanied by a recognition of political equality?" he asked. "Chattels personal may be instantly translated from the auction block to freedman, but when were they ever taken at the same time to the ballot box, and invested with all political rights and immunities?" According to the "laws of development and progress," Garrison declared, immediate political equality for emancipated slaves was simply "not practicable." He had taken the same position on the franchise in 1831.

Since Christian assistance and uplift of the "perishing bondsman" had numbered high among the original tenets of the American Anti-Slavery Society, Garrison deeply resented Phillips's charge that he was betraying his abolitionist commitment by upholding this doctrine now. To Phillips, however, Garrison's stress on philanthropy offered only "an old clothes movement" that would "dish out thin soup" to the freed people while remanding their fates to custody of vengeful white planters. "Our nation owes the negro not merely freedom," Phillips emphasized. "It owes him land; it owes him the ballot; it owes him education also. It is a debt that will disgrace us before the people if we do not pay it." Garrison could see no reason to worry about "disgrace," or to wonder what Phillips meant by the term "merely freedom." As newspapers across the North speculated on the growing rift between Garrison and Phillips, both antagonists did try to keep up appearances by issuing denials and treating each other respectfully in public. In private, however, the pain of severing a quarter century of friendship quickly began to surface as deep resentment. Phillips, for example, angrily cancelled his subscription to the *Liberator* and the *National Anti-Slavery Standard*, furious over their pro-Lincoln editorials. "I would rather have severed my right hand," he told a friend, "than write pro-Lincoln articles" as Garrison did. Garrison, for his part, began taking pains to avoid meeting with Phillips at all. There were "breakers ahead," he warned *Standard* editor Oliver Johnson. "I fear P. has made up his mind to leave us. . . . He is evidently in a heated state." Soon after, while Phillips attended a Massachusetts Republican party convention as a Frémont delegate in June 1864, Garrison traveled triumphantly to Baltimore to witness Lincoln's renomination. It was a trip that would confirm as nothing else could his perception of personal triumph.

In Baltimore, Garrison found a complete fusion of his earliest memories of solitary struggle with this present sense of imminent victory. As if to highlight this dramatic fulfillment of past prophesies with current developments, he chose as his traveling companions the aging George Thompson, his mob-tried British compatriot from the early 1830s, and Theodore Tilden, the powerful young editor. As the three of them sat in the gallery observing the activities of the Republican convention, the chair of the proceedings announced Garrison's presence, and as he moved among the delegates later, "all hats went off, all hands were thrust out in welcome, and all hospitable manners" were directed toward him. By the end, not only the delegates but the Republican party's platform as well had confirmed to Garrison beyond all doubt that he had, indeed, finally been "HEARD." The party, he wrote Helen, had given "a full endorsement of all the abolitionist 'fanaticism' and 'incendiarism' with which I stood branded for all these years." The proceedings, he assured her, "have been such as to gladden my heart, and almost make me fear I am at home dreaming, and not in the state of Maryland."

As if to confirm that his triumphs were not merely fantasy, Garrison lingered in Baltimore following the convention to refresh his memories of youthful struggle. As he did so he doubtless recalled with deep satisfaction his mother's deathbed skepticism over his choice of career and his determination, nonetheless, to seek worldly fame and moral sanctification as a "self-made" editorialist. He searched in vain, however, for the old jail in which he had been incarcerated for libelling Francis Todd, and from which he had emerged to begin his work with the *Liberator*. Though the jail had been torn down years before, Garrison prevailed on the clerk to check the city register for surviving jurors, and when eight were identified, the presiding judge jokingly offered to convene a new trial. Though deprived of the chance to read the sonnet he had penned on his cell wall so many years before, Garrison clearly could be satisfied that he had achieved his most enduring ambitions.

If Baltimore confirmed for Garrison his mastery over the past, his next stop, Washington, convinced him of his prominence in the present. Senator Henry Wilson had arranged interviews for him with President Lincoln, as well as with influential Cabinet members such as Secretary of War Edwin Stanton and Secretary of the Treasury Salmon P. Chase. At a White House reception Lincoln greeted Garrison most cordially, set up a formal interview for the following day, and introduced him to his other guests. "I was at once surrounded with a larger group of guests than even [Lincoln] himself," he told Helen proudly. Next, Garrison met privately with Stanton, "a man of thorough-going anti-slavery spirit," and mingled on the Senate floor with other Republican luminaries who were eager to shake his hand. The following day, Lincoln and Garrison met for an hour-long interview, a "very satisfactory one indeed," in Garrison's opinion. Garrison made plain his intentions to stand by Lincoln against the Frémont insurgency, and the President replied that he was counting on the abolitionists' support and discussed some of his plans for reconstruction. Lincoln's friendliness and apparent candor, the "familiar. . .way in which he unbosomed himself," won Garrison over completely. He left Washington convinced that the President was determined to "uproot slavery and give fair play to the emancipated," and felt satisfied that his advice had influence in the highest councils of the nation. Republican leaders, in turn, regarded Garrison's support as a valuable endorsement of their party's moral high-mindedness and heroic mission. As the *Philadelphia Press*, a powerful Lincoln newspaper, observed, "whatever William Lloyd Garrison says has weight. He is still as he has been for thirty years, the leader of the American Abolitionists. Mr. Garrison, in sustaining Mr. Lincoln, proves conclusively that the Presi-

dent is not the candidate of the weak—semi-proslavery conservative faction."

The 1864 presidential election proved Garrison, for once, an
accurate political prognosticator. Despite Phillips's verbal assaults on Lincoln, or perhaps in part because of them, Frémont's bid for office collapsed in confusion and the President
easily gained reelection. But while Garrison judged the victory
a tribute to the "honesty, sagacity, administrative ability and patriotic integrity of Abraham Lincoln," he also knew that the
results portended a final and definitive struggle with Phillips
over the disbanding of the American Anti-Slavery Society and
the meaning of the abolitionist crusade. In his own mind, the
moment for declaring success was coming ever closer, for with
Lincoln's position secure, Congress immediately considered a
constitutional amendment abolishing slavery. This, of course,
was Garrison's final requirement for achieving full victory. By
February 1865, the Thirteenth Amendment had been passed
and submitted to the states for its inevitable ratification, and
Garrison declared the day of "Jubilee" to be imminent. "LAUS
DEO!—HALLELUJAH" he trumpeted in the *Liberator*, hailing the
event as "the most important . . . in the history of congressional
legislation." To a hastily assembled but overflowing Grand Jubilee
Meeting in Boston's Music Hall, Garrison proclaimed the triumph
of abolitionism and a complete justification of every principle undergirding his long career. The extract moment to terminate his
and the nation's quest for emancipation was now at hand:

> At last, after eighty years of wandering and darkness,—of cruelty
> and oppression, on a colossal scale, towards a helpless and an unof-
> fending race—of recreancy to all the Heaven-attested principles
> enunciated by our revolutionary sires in justification of their course;
> through righteous judgement and fiery retribution; through na-
> tional dismemberment and civil war; through suffering, bereave-
> ment and lamentation, extending to every city, town, village and
> hamlet, almost every household in the land; through a whole gener-
> ation of Anti-Slavery warning, expostulation and rebuke, resulting

in wide spread contrition and repentance; the nation, rising in the majesty of its moral power and political sovereignty, has decreed that LIBERTY shall be "PROCLAIMED THROUGHOUT ALL THE LAND, TO ALL THE INHABITANTS THEREOF,: and that henceforth no such anomalous being as slaveholder or slave shall exist beneath the "stars and stripes," within the domains of the republic.

Judged in this moment of exhilaration, Garrison's recent experiences seemed to have led him from one vindicating drama after another. In Baltimore he had fused his memories of his obscure past with his sense of victory by seeking out his jail cell and mingling with prominent Republicans. Next, in Washington, Lincoln himself had assured him that his counsel helped determine the nation's destiny, a fact now confirmed by Lincoln's reelection and the passage of the Thirteenth Amendment. All that remained now to complete the ritual of Garrison's fulfillment was confirmation of their freedom from the former slaves themselves, because for thirty years Garrison's personal quest for liberation from his own conflicting desires for purity and power had been tied inextricably to their emancipation. When the occasion presented itself to witness these fruits of abolition firsthand, Garrison eagerly seized the opportunity.

Garrison revealed his plan to visit South Carolina in a carefully contrived drama that recalled his burning of the Constitution in 1854. In early April 1865, just after General Ulysses S. Grant had captured the Confederate capital of Richmond, Virginia, Garrison arranged a freedman's aid meeting in Chelsea, Massachusetts. The decor of that occasion featured a slave auction block next to the podium, the steps to which were draped with a Confederate flag captured by the 55th Massachusetts Regiment, an African American fighting unit to which Garrison's son, George Thompson Garrison, was attached. When the hall had filled, Garrison mounted the platform and read a telegram from Secretary of War Edwin Stanton. It invited him to be the government's official guest at a flag-raising ceremony at Fort Sumter on April 14, an event meant to memorialize the fifth anniversary of the outbreak of the war. As the crowd responded enthusiastically, Garrison expanded at length on the thought that visiting South Carolina, hotbed of secession, would demonstrate as could no other experience "that slavery is annihilated beyond any hope of resurrection."

Anxious to meet the former slaves whose emancipation was synonymous with his own, Garrison boarded ship for Charleston on April 7, 1865. The voyage was a delight for Garrison. He mingled with the judges, ministers, editors, and businessmen who made up the official delegation, and was pleased to report to Helen that all of them agreed with his views on reconstruction. Moreover, the ship arrived in Charleston harbor on the same morning as the electrifying news of the Confederate surrender to Grant at Appomattox Courthouse. By noon, as victory celebrations were breaking out everywhere, the party reached Fort Sumter and debarked for a ceremony that featured a moving speech by Major General Robert T. Anderson, the federal commander who had been forced to surrender the installation in 1861. When the Union flag was raised over the fort, volleys of cannon fire shook the harbor and everyone "grasped hands, shouted and wept for joy." Following the ceremony, everyone reconvened in the Charleston Hotel to partake of a celebration dinner and a major speech by William Lloyd Garrison.

Garrison took the podium to contrast the years 1835 and 1865, dates which allowed him to frame out the full flowering of his crusade. Then, he had been mobbed in "freedom-loving" Boston. Now, he observed, he was being cheered in "secessionist" Charleston, and the transformation showed that "we are living in altered times. To me it is something like the translation from death to life—from the cerements of the grave to the robes of Heaven," his sense of personal rebirth now wholly fused with the reality of slave emancipation. He reminisced, too, about his imprisonment in Baltimore in 1829 for defending the "helpless slave." Now, he proclaimed, "Maryland has adopted Garrisonian Abolitionism and accepted a Constitution endorsing every principle I have advocated on behalf of the slave." Even the President of the United States embraced the abolitionist cause, Garrison proclaimed happily: "Either he has become a Garrisonian Abolitionist or I have become a Lincoln Emancipationist, for . . . we blend together, like kindred drops, into one." Thus did Garrison announce himself at peace with the nation whose values he had so long decried, and that had for so long rejected him as a dangerous fanatic.

The next day, a mass meeting of freed African Americans gave Garrison a thrilling ratification of the ending of his war with slavery. A crowd estimated at ten thousand assembled outside the Charleston Citadel, and when Garrison appeared the freed people and their white supporters seized him joyfully and bore him around the square. Charleston's Superintendent of Public Instruction then introduced him to two thousand African American schoolchildren who greeted him with cheers, after which they and their parents escorted him to Zion's Church where he was asked to speak. A former slave introduced Garrison with polished formality by pointing to his own two neatly dressed daughters: "Now, Sir, through your labors and those of your noble co-agitators, these are mine. No man can take them from me. Accept these flowers as a token of our gratitude and love . . . as a simple offering from those for whom you have done so much." Garrison, deeply touched, responded in the same accents of Christian utopianism that had always both inspired and constricted his vision of black freedom: "It was not on account of your complexion or race, as a people, that I espoused your cause, but because you were children of a common Father, created in the same divine image, having the same inalienable rights, and as much entitled to liberty as the proudest slaveholder that ever walked on the face of the earth."

Not long after, the affairs of the American Anti-Slavery Society played themselves out to a predictable conclusion. Anticipating titanic struggles between Garrison and his opponents, most of abolitionism's leading figures attended the annual meeting, and hot debates filled two entire days. Even the deep uncertainty and grief caused by Lincoln's tragic assassination could not make Garrison question his conviction that the Thirteenth

Amendment had "spiked the guns" of the American Anti-
Slavery Society. "Let us mingle with the millions of our fellow
countrymen in one common effort to establish justice and liberty throughout the land," he declared as he offered resolutions
to dissolve the organization. When his motion lost, 118–48, Garrison declined the nominating committee's generous offer to in-
stall him as president despite the adverse vote. Phillips assumed
the position instead and Garrison bid his colleagues an "affectionate adieu." "My vocation as an abolitionist is ended," he assured Oliver Johnson privately, and so, it turned out, were the
careers of most of his closest supporters. Except for Phillips,
nearly every leader of the Boston clique who had not already
done so followed Garrison into retirement, notably Quincy,
Samuel J. May, and Oliver Johnson.

Those who remained with Phillips to continue the battle for
black male suffrage and southern land redistribution came from
every stratum of the antebellum crusade against slavery, and
most were veterans in their fifties and sixties who had already
given decades of service to "the cause." Gerrit Smith and John
Greenleaf Whittier, both evangelicals with Liberty party backgrounds, now served as vice presidents of the American Anti-
Slavery Society. Longstanding anticlericals and political
extremists like the Fosters, Pillsbury, Henry C. Wright, and
Charles C. Burleigh also stayed with Phillips, as did a formidable contingent of African American leaders—Douglass, Remond, Purvis, and George Downing to name only the most
prominent. So did Elizabeth Cady Stanton, Lucretia Mott, and
Susan B. Anthony, who increasingly equated the demand for
black male enfranchisement with feminist causes.

For the next several years, these persistent militants continued
to demand racial justice by linking the ballot with the goal of social equality. Their particular abolitionist crusade would not
conclude until 1870, when the Fifteenth Amendment extended
the franchise to all the nation's adult males, American Indians
excepted. In league with Republican politicians in Congress,
members of the American Anti-Slavery Society also demanded

a complete remaking of the South as a biracial democracy. The might of the Union Army, they insisted, must be deployed to protect the rights of African Americans. Land and education must also be furnished to the freed people to secure for them the exercise of their citizenship. Of course, for the retired Garrison, as for all his now-vindicated colleagues, such a program meant granting to freed people not basic rights, but unearned privileges. As one who believed he had fulfilled his every dream as a self-made man, Garrison still felt that striving independently for success, not relying on others for special favors, should be the only way to secure black citizenship. The coercion proposed by Phillips, he emphasized, "would gain nothing" for "universal suffrage and will be hard to win and to hold without a general preparation of feeling and sentiment." Only "by struggle *on the part of the disenfranchised*" would justice for all finally arrive "in the good times coming." Secure in these opinions, Garrison embarked on a farewell speaking tour and on December 29, 1865, when the news arrived that the Thirteenth Amendment had been ratified, printed up the final issue of the *Liberator*. As to the future of slaves, he declared in his final editorial, he was now content to leave "what remains to be done to complete the work of emancipation to other instrumentalities (of which I hope to avail myself)," particularly the philanthropy of the Freedmen's Aid Societies.

Garrison's hope, though sincere, quickly proved fleeting. Beginning in 1866 momentous struggles over Southern reconstruction policy developed between the Republican-dominated Congress and Lincoln's successor as President, Andrew Johnson. Believing that the fundamental issues raised by the war could never be resolved by simply emancipating the slaves and then readmitting the rebel states, most Republicans, not just true radicals like Phillips or Sumner, now called for stringent federal protection for the political rights of the former slaves. In several strongly worded speeches and in articles for Tilden's *Independent*, Garrison encouraged the Republican majority in Congress to defy Andrew Johnson's obstructionism and take steps themselves to protect former slaves from white intimidation. He also served briefly as president of the Freedmen's Aid Society, which supported education for southern blacks. But otherwise, he remained largely aloof from the struggles of Radical Reconstruction that preoccupied the nation throughout the later 1860s. While debate went forward over civil rights legislation, the military occupation of the South, and additional constitutional amendments to guarantee freed people's rights, Garrison added a supportive voice but played no prominent role. Instead, he embarked on a nostalgic tour of England, leaving to others the struggles over the enactment of the Fourteenth Amendment and the proposed impeachment of Andrew Johnson.

When Garrison returned to the United States in October 1867 he discovered, much to his delight, that his friends and admirers were far more anxious to remember his past achievements than to seek his guidance on current affairs. Leading figures from all walks of life had begun establishing a fund to support his retirement, giving him all the confirmation he ever needed as to the glorious conclusion of his public career. Knowing that Garrison's income was far from ample, merchant-abolitionist Henry Bowditch, former Massachusetts governor John A. Andrew, Quincy, May, and several other prominent supporters had formed a committee to raise a substantial retirement fund as a national testimonial to Garrison's lifelong labors on behalf of the slave. Nearly all of Garrison's oldest allies and even some of his bitterest former antagonists agreed to head the list of subscribers—Gerrit Smith, the Westons, Samuel May, Jr., Lydia Maria Child, Whittier, Samuel Sewell, and Samuel J. May. Other contributions and endorsers included Stanton and Seward from the Cabinet, Supreme Court Chief Justice Chase, Senators Sumner and Wilson, dozens of wealthy businessmen and several luminaries of American literature, notably Ralph Waldo Emerson, James Russell Lowell, and Henry Wadsworth Longfellow—a veritable "blue book" of the north's most influential and respected people. The poor and unrecognized added their testimonials, too. An African American domestic servant, for example, sent with her single dollar the thought that "If I were a milionaire [sic] by the Gods' I would give him 1,000,000. and make him President of the United States. When he dies his destiny is in the Heaven of Heavens." By May 1870, with over $35,000 collected on his behalf, Garrison's finances were to remain ample for the rest of his life. His reputation unsullied, his assurance of moral virtue complete, and his pride in personal independence just as strong as ever, he accepted with pleasure this powerful tribute as "the leader and inspirer of the movement against slavery." "Of this testimonial," he stressed in his statement of acceptance, "none was ever more unsought or unexpected; none more spontaneous or more honorable was ever proffered." Content to be sustained by financial support of others, Garrison remained fully satisfied that his were the well-earned rewards of a truly self-made man.

Retirement treated Garrison kindly. Thanks to his connection with editor Theodore Tilden, the *Independent* welcomed his contributions, and until the mid-1870s he continued to air his opinions on temperance, women's rights, peace, medical issues, and labor questions. He remained healthy despite two bone-breaking falls and his persistent hypochondriac worries, although rheumatism gave him increasing problems. He occasionally attended gatherings of reformers, where he always felt welcome and was treated with respect though he seldom had much to say. On several such occasions his path crossed Phillips's from whom he still remained deeply estranged. Nevertheless his old associate saw clearly just how happy Garrison was in his declining years, how secure in his sense of fulfillment. "It was very pleasant," Phillips remarked to his wife, Anne. "I saw Garrison in the hall as he came in. I am very glad his life is ending so happily. He seems wholly at rest." Almost until the day he died, Phillips was to remain the unsatisfied militant, contending until the last not only for racial equality but for the rights of working-class people across the nation. Never able to believe in the substance of his own great achievements, Phillips was acutely aware and not a little envious that Garrison had achieved such a deep inner peace.

Eventually, even Garrison's memories of his angry parting with Phillips began to ease. They kept meeting at the gravesites of co-workers, sharing responsibilities for the conduct of Samuel J. May's funeral in 1871 and Henry C. Wright's in 1875. Phillips grieved openly with Garrison over such losses, and Garrison began sending Anne Phillips jars of his homemade jam. Stimulated by the revival of this old and dearest friendship, Garrison joined Phillips in 1875 to speak out strongly in support of Charles Sumner's Civil Rights Act, a sweeping piece of legislation designed to outlaw racial segregation throughout the United States. It finally passed in weakened form soon after Sumner's death. And in 1876, when his beloved Helen died, a desolate Garrison turned instinctively to Phillips for consolation and support. Grieving too deeply to attend the funeral, Garrison relied on Phillips to officiate and deliver the eulogy. Soon after, as a token of appreciation, Garrison sent Phillips a memoir of the abolitionist movement he had written in Helen's honor, and the orator, genuinely moved, replied that the gift "takes me back so many years—and brings back to memory so many dear names—the memories of our toilsome, triumphant day."

Without Helen, Garrison had few supports left for sustaining day-to-day living. As his own health began to fail, friends persuaded him that another trip to England and the Continent might bring restoration, but he returned exhausted and saddened by his final parting from George Thompson. Preferring to attend living-room seances through which he attempted to communicate with Helen and other departed dear ones, Garrison chose to remain at home. Visits from grandchildren buoyed his spirits, as did a special pilgrimage he made to Newburyport in 1878 to visit the old *Herald* office where he had first learned the printer's trade nearly seventy years before. As he set three sonnets into type, he noted with satisfaction that the young apprentices were amazed at his flawless accuracy and speed. From there he traveled to Boston where the Franklin Club, an association of young printers and apprentices, gave a dinner in his honor. To the end, Garrison could never resist reminding himself of how far he had risen from his humble origins.

As his health failed, his worried daughter Fanny insisted that Garrison move to her home in New York City. Soon after his arrival in April 1879, kidney failure sent him into complete invalidism, and as he lingered semiconscious for nearly a month everyone knew the end was near. All his family gathered at his bedside, and in the evenings they sang the hymns he had taught them as children while with eyes closed he marked time with his hand. On May 22, the attending physician inquired of Garrison if there was anything he wanted. "To finish it up," he replied softly. Garrison lapsed into a deep coma the next day, and shortly thereafter it was indeed finished.

EPILOGUE

Judgments

By his own estimate, Garrison's career concluded in unqualified victory. Hailed after the war as the nation's foremost liberator, he felt so secure about his place in history that he spurned all suggestions that he write his autobiography. Four million emancipated blacks seemed to him proof beyond question that the nation had moved into a new era of freedom and that he would always be remembered for inspiring this achievement. But subsequent events, as we know, failed to confirm Garrison's expectations. When he died in 1879, southern reconstruction was already ending in disaster and white supremacy had begun reasserting its strength throughout the nation.

In the old Confederacy, vigilantism, lynching, and disenfranchisement brought forth oppressive new systems of sharecropping and segregation. In the North, the drive for racial justice was soon blunted by a growing belief in the "survival of the fittest" that gave powerful new support for white supremacy. In the year of his death, it was becoming all too clear that Garrison's claims of victory were, at best, questionable, for the moral revolution that was to have reconciled the races had never come to pass. A titanic political struggle between antagonistic cultures based on free and slave labor, not the egalitarian vision of Garrisonian saints, had resulted in the war and emancipation. Union armies, not immediate abolitionists, had finally shattered the relationship between master and slave. Because white America's values were essentially unchanged, slave emancipation led nearly at once to new and intractable forms of racial oppression.

What meaning, then, should be assigned to Garrison's life in light of this continuing history of racial tragedy? One might well present the argument that Garrison himself must bear heavy responsibility. His perfectionist attacks on slavery, one might suggest, dealt far too much in moral absolutes and abstractions, far too little in workable solutions to the tangled problems of slavery and racism. To this, one might add the criticisms that Garrison's racial paternalism and obsessive devotion to romantic individualism blinded him to the deeper challenges of a society built on white supremacy and competitive capitalism. Finally, one might observe that Garrison's preoccupation with self-purity isolated him from the political process that finally defined the terms of black emancipation. Far from acting as the nation's conscience, he never was able to provide meaningful guidance to those who finally legislated the direction of race relations.

Each of these assessments has been put forward and addressed in the foregoing pages and readers should carefully weigh their merit. Yet, as this study also suggests, it is not sufficient to judge Garrison's career a failure because of a discouraging aftermath where racism prevailed. Indeed, it is vital to remember that Garrison himself ceaselessly warned that exactly such a destiny awaited America in the absence of the moral revolution for which he crusaded. His demand that the nation transform its racist values was certainly utopian. In the end, perhaps for that reason, it was a demand that Garrison, too, compromised for the sake of his own sense of vindication. Nonetheless, his Christian formulations of racial egalitarianism and his calls for moral revolution can be seen as constituting a comprehensive, compelling challenge to Americans of his generation. Understanding how and why that generation responded as it did yields, perhaps, the most accurate measure of Garrison's importance.

Was the nation's failure to address the problem of race the result of flaws in Garrison's vision or motives? Was that failure instead to some degree the result of the nation's deeper incapacity to respond creatively to Garrison's insightful challenge? In addressing these questions it should hardly surprise us to learn that Garrison, bound by the limitations of place and time, could not transform the culture that had shaped him and was unable to discern the ultimate consequences of his actions. We should, however, be prepared to explain why so many white Americans before the Civil War proved unable to gain some deeper wisdom from his crusade. And likewise, we should also be able to account for the fact that many of Garrison's colleagues and other contemporaries genuinely found him to be an authentic liberator. Whatever his limitations, or whatever the larger failure of his generation, his war against slavery did provoke men and women of both races to sharpen their vision of social justice and seek a much fuller realization of American democracy. For this reason, if for no other, Garrison's career should continue to enrich our historical perspectives as we face the continuing tragedy of racial oppression in our own time.

BIBLIOGRAPHICAL ESSAY

Our historical perspectives will become all the clearer by considering how other historians, apart from this study, have assessed the meaning of Garrison's career. Garrison's earliest biographers were his contemporaries, and they were eager to insure the historical vindication for their subject. Francis Jackson Garrison and Wendell Phillips Garrison's *William Lloyd Garrison* (1879) therefore stressed their father's quintessential role as the guiding spirit of the antislavery crusade, presenting him as a reformer with faultless vision, selflessly dedicated to humanity's betterment and the nation's moral uplift. Oliver Johnson's *William Lloyd Garrison and His Times* (1881) and Samuel J. May's *Some Recollections of Our Anti-Slavery Conflict* (1869) offered the same accolades, but by the opening of the twentieth century, assessments of Garrison's life became far more hostile. The growing influence of white supremacy in American historical thought led a number of scholars to dismiss opposition to slavery as a form of neurotic behavior and to charge abolitionists such as Garrison with needlessly inflaming the planter class. From this perspective, Garrison's career was hardly worth examining and no biography was written during the first five decades of the twentieth century. However, characterizations of Garrison as irresponsible or deeply disturbed can be sampled in Hazel Wolf, *On Freedom's Altar* (1952) and Avery Craven, *The Coming of the Civil War* (1950). A much more valuable study, unique for its time, which treats abolitionists in general as serious religious thinkers and social activists but which also portrays Garrison as neurotically destructive to "the cause' is Gilbert Hobbes Barnes, *The Anti-Slavery Impulse, 1831–1860* (1934).

Modern treatment of Garrison's life began with two works from the 1950s, both deeply influenced by the nascent civil rights movement and by the damaging impact of McCarthyism on civil liberties. Both Ralph Korngold, *Two Friends of Man: The Story of William Lloyd Garrison and Wendell Phillips and Their Relationship with Abraham Lincoln* (1950) and Russell B. Nye, *William Lloyd Garrison and the Humanitarian Reformers* (1955) treat Garrison as a substantial leader who defended freedom of expression and advanced the cause of racial justice. Many of the same judgments are reflected in Walter M. Merrill's deeply researched *Against Wind and Tide: A Biography of William Lloyd Garrison* (1965), the most detailed of all renderings of Garrison's life and one that treats his private foibles forthrightly despite its general sympathy for its subject.

John L. Thomas's *The Liberator: William Lloyd Garrison, A Biography* (1963) still stands as the most challenging and searching of all Garrison's portrayals to date. Influenced by the "American studies" scholarship of the 1950s, as well as by the early civil rights movement, Thomas takes the moral issue of slavery very seriously and presents Garrison as shaped by a Jacksonian cultural ethos of unrestrained, romantic individualism. Garrison, as presented by Thomas, embodied an insatiably egocentric self-consciousness who felt compelled to defy authority and shun collective responsibility for slavery in pursuit of his own inner perfection. By developing Garrison's biography so fully in its cultural setting while refusing to slight the moral problems of slavery, Thomas's study retains much of its currency even in the face of a quarter-century of revisionist scholarship. Its influence, in fact, can even be discerned in a very recent interpretation of Garrison's motivation offered by R. Jackson Wilson in a chapter in his *Figures of Speech: American Writers and the Literary Marketplace from Benjamin Franklin to Emily Dickinson* (1989). In this highly focussed essay, Wilson, like Thomas, portrays Garrison as a self-absorbed, transcendence-seeking individualist. But unlike Thomas, Wilson attributes those characteristics far less to Garrison's religiosity per se or to the explicit relationship between his drive for prophetic self-purification and the moral challenges of slavery. Instead, Wilson emphasizes the influence of Garrison's turbulent early years, particularly his relationship with his mother, which compelled his lifelong effort to secure literary fame as a self-made man by adopting a posture of defiance. Wilson's analysis, like Thomas's, offers provocative insights on Garrison's personal makeup that have influenced my own treatment of his motivation.

Stanley Elkins, Wilson's colleague at Smith College, has been as influential as any other historian in portraying Garrison as a self-preoccupied individualist. Though Elkins's *Slavery: A Problem in American Institutional and Intellectual Life* (1959) preceded Wilson's essay by over thirty years, the two works can certainly be read as complementing one another. Informed by a suspicion of extremist ideology that characterized much historical thinking in the 1950s, Elkins pointed to Garrison as embodying the fatal weakness of pre–Civil War America's unrestrained approaches to race reform. To Elkins, the essence of Garrison's failure, and that of his generation, was a narcissistic preoccupation with individual sin and guilt caused by an unremitting hostility to established institutions and an utter disinterest in incremental approaches to ending slavery. Wilson's portrayal of Garrison the solitary seeker of fame in the marketplace of ideas, Thomas's of Garrison the untrammelled religious romantic, and Elkins's portrait of Garrison the rootless transcendentalist combine to create a general picture of Garrison as an alienated individualist driven by insatiable inner needs and detached from the social and political realities of his time.

Before long, however, these skeptical views of Garrison and the abolitionists came under attack from scholars who welcomed ideological conflict for the cause of social justice. By the mid 1960s a flourishing civil rights movement was inspiring a new group of scholars who called themselves "neoabolitionists" and defended Garrison and the abolitionists from doubters such as Thomas and Elkins. The best representation of this scholarship, which argues vigorously and trenchantly for the clarity of Garrison's reform vision and the appropriateness of his agitator's approach is Aileen Kraditor, *Means and Ends in American Abolitionism: Garrison and his Critics on Strategy and Tactics* (1969). In Kraditor's view, Garrison's suspicion of American institutions was an insightful response to a racist society, not a romantic expression of abstracted self-absorption. His preachments on sin and guilt challenged the nation to face its collective responsibility for race oppression rather than simply reflecting his conscience-stricken individualism. His decision to spurn conventional politics bespoke a clear understanding of the pitfalls of electoral compromise, not an exercise in self-righteous disengagement. An interpretive *tour de force*, Kraditor's richly documented analysis, which has informed my work at many points, has insured that Garrison will never again be characterized as simply a self-preoccupied purist or the flawed embodiment of an individualistic age. Other elaborations of neoabolitionist interpretation can be found in Martin Duberman, ed., *The Anti-Slavery Vanguard* (1965) and Carleton Mabee, *The Non-Violent Abolitionists* (1970).

From this neoabolitionist perspective, Wilson's recent picture of Garrison as a solitary, defiant writer more anxious for personal fulfillment than for black emancipation might well seem to herald a return to the older views of Elkins and Thomas. Actually, Wilson's interpretations reflect some of the more current trends in historical thinking. Since the mid-1970s, as the optimism of the civil rights movement has waned, so has the confidence of many scholars in the substance of Garrison's leadership and in the abolitionists' pertinence as racial reformers. One consequence of this shift has been to redefine abolitionism as embodying the dominant trends of an emerging market-based culture of Victorian capitalism rather than as a truly radical rebellion against caste oppression. A second result has been to emphasize increasingly the racist tendencies of white abolitionists such as Garrison, a view that also stresses their commonality with, not their struggles against, the dominant values of their age. A final consequence of this renewed historical skepticism has led to an emphasis on the importance of the personal significance of the abolitionist commitment to the lives of the crusaders themselves. This view suggests strongly that the reformers' overriding desire was to achieve self-fulfillment, not dramatic social change.

Each of these judgments accords in some measure with those of Wilson, Thomas, and Elkins, marking some clear departures from neoabolitionist thinking. Such scholarship is especially well exemplified in Ronald Walters's *The Antislavery Appeal: American Abolitionism After* 1830 (1976) and his *American Reformers* (1978); two studies by Lawrence J. Friedman, *Inventors of the Promised Land* (1975) and *Gregarious Saints: Self and Community in American Abolitionism,* 1830–1870 (1982); and Louis Gerteis, *Morality and Utility in Antislavery Reform* (1987). Meanwhile, scholars who continue to find value in "neoabolitionist" perspectives include James Brewer Stewart, *Holy Warriors: The Abolitionists and American Slavery* (1976) and *Wendell Phillips: Liberty's Hero* (1986); Merton Dillon, *The Abolitionists: The Growth of a Dissenting Minority* (1974) and John R. McKivigan, *The War Against Proslavery Religion: Abolitionism and Northern Churches,* 1830–1865 (1984).

Readers wishing a more complete understanding of these shifts in interpretation and of the historiography of abolitionism generally should consult these fine articles: Betty L. Fladeland, "Revisionists vs. Abolitionists: The Historiographical Cold War of the 1930s and 1940s," *Journal of the Early Republic* (1986), 1–21; Lawrence J. Friedman "Historical Topics Southern Run Dry: The State of Abolitionist Studies," *The Historian* (February 1981), 177–94; Merton Dillon, "The Abolitionists: A Decade of Historiography, 1959–1969," *Journal of Southern History* (December 1969), 76–93; Richard O. Curry and Lawrence Goodheart, "Knives in Their Heads: Passionate Self-Analysis and the Search for Identity in Recent Abolitionist Historiography," *Canadian Journal of American Studies* (1983), 401–14. An extraordinarily good introduction to the social and political environment in which abolitionism took root is Harry L. Watson, *Liberty and Power: The Politics of Jacksonian America* (1990).

The surest way to form well-founded judgments on Garrison and the abolitionists is, of course, to examine the original sources. Fortunately, the most important of these are numerous and easy to obtain. Walter M. Merrill and Louis Ruchames, eds., *The Letters of William Lloyd Garrison, 1805–1879,* 5 vols. (1970–79), reproduce with detailed annotation nearly every important letter that Garrison ever wrote. Francis Jackson Garrison and Wendell Phillips Garrison also published a wealth of their father's correspondence and editorial writings in *William Lloyd Garrison, 1805–1879,* 4 vols. (1885–89). The memoirs of James Holley Garrison, Garrison's brother, have been edited by Walter M. Merrill in *Behold Myself Once More* (1959) and contain reprints of very valuable letters by Fanny Lloyd Garrison. The *Liberator* and the *National Anti-Slavery Standard* are available on microfilm through interlibrary loan, as are most leading abolitionist newspapers. In addition, Claire Taylor, *British and American Abolitionists: An Episode in Transatlantic Understanding* (1974) reprints much correspondence between reformers on both sides of the Atlantic. Other important published collections of primary documents include Gilbert Hobbes Barnes and Dwight L. Dumond, eds., *The Letters of Theodore Dwight Weld, Angelina Grimké Weld and Sarah Grimké, 1822–1844,* 2 vols., (1941); Dwight L. Dumond, *The Letters of James Gillespie Birney, 1831–1857* (1938); John Blassingame, John McKivigan, et al., eds., *The Frederick Douglass Papers,* Vols. 1 and 2 (1979, 1982); Peter Ripley et al., eds., *The Black Abolitionist Papers,* vols. 1–3 (1984–89); Philip Foner, ed., *The Life and Writings of Frederick Douglass* (1950–55), and Irving Bartlett, ed., *Wendell and Ann Phillips and the Community of Reform* (1984). Good anthologies of abolitionist writings, easy to obtain, which reproduce a wide variety of shorter selections include John L. Thomas, ed., *Slavery Attacked* (1965); Louis Ruchames, ed., *The Abolitionists* (1964); Truman Nelson, ed., *Documents of Upheaval: Selections from* The Liberator (1966); Herbert Aptheker, ed., *Documentary History of the Negro People,* vol. 1 (1968); and William H. and Jane H. Pease, eds., *The Antislavery Argument* (1965).

INDEX